Learning Adobe Connect 9

Successfully create and host web meetings, virtual classes, and webinars with Adobe Connect

Miloš Radovanović

Miloš Vučetić

PUBLISHING

BIRMINGHAM - MUMBAI

Learning Adobe Connect 9

First published: April 2013

Production Reference: 1160413

Published by Packt Publishing Ltd.
Livery Place
35 Livery Street
Birmingham B3 2PB, UK.

ISBN 978-1-84969-416-2

www.packtpub.com

Cover Image by Laura Garton (laurahg123@hotmail.co.uk)

Credits

Authors
Miloš Radovanović

Miloš Vučetić

Reviewer
Laurent Janolin

Acquisition Editor
Wilson D'souza

Commissioning Editor
Priyanka S

Technical Editors
Kaustubh S. Mayekar

Devdutt Kulkarni

Copy Editors
Laxmi Subramanian

Brandt D'Mello

Alfida Paiva

Project Coordinator
Esha Thakker

Proofreader
Lawrence A. Herman

Indexer
Hemangini Bari

Production Coordinator
Aparna Bhagat

Nitesh Thakur

Cover Work
Aparna Bhagat

About the Authors

Miloš Radovanović is a software engineer at software powerhouse PSTech in Belgrade, Serbia, where he dedicates most of his time to working on projects related to the Adobe Connect application. His daily love affair involves passionate development of various Adobe Connect components on the backend side, with occasional road trips to the frontend. His engineering skills are extended across a multitude of exciting world-renowned platforms and technologies including Java, MySQL, Eclipse, Ant, Hibernate, Spring, and Flex. He began his life-changing journey with the Adobe Connect application as a quality automation engineer where he was exposed to all the marvelous application features.

He graduated from the University of Belgrade, with an M.Sc. in Applied Mathematics. In addition to being completely dedicated to his work, he loves soccer, snowboarding, and the incredible sounds of house music. He lives in Belgrade, Serbia, with his beloved wife, Nataša.

I would like to thank my greatest inspiration, Ksenija (my soon to be born baby daughter) and my wife, Nataša, who is very proud of me for completing this book. She was always there for me with unreserved support and encouragement while working on the book.

Additionally, I would like to thank my parents for helping me overcome many difficulties and to endure many challenges in life. Last but not least, my special thanks goes to my friend and colleague Miloš Vučetić, who is the coauthor of this book and my everyday partner in the Adobe Connect engineering adventures, and to Gabriele Giganti, who helped tremendously with his advice, which helped my self-esteem in the moments when I had my doubts about completing this book.

Miloš Vučetić is a software engineer at software development company PSTech in Belgrade, Serbia. Miloš connected with the Adobe Connect application for the first time as a quality automation engineer, where his passion for in-depth code testing introduced him to the magnificent features of this great application. He continued his work on the application on the creative side by developing various components for Connect, along with a large bundle of third-party tools that integrate perfectly with Adobe Connect due to his never-ending quest for perfection and quality. His artistic soul continues to expand horizons, as he uses Flex and Java to continue his great works of programming and further enhance users' visual and functional experience with Connect. In his everyday enterprise adventures, he uses multiple technologies and platforms to improve every aspect of his development skills. He graduated from the University of Belgrade, with a B.A. in Information Systems and Technologies. He lives with his girlfriend, Zorica, in Belgrade, who occasionally lets him play cards with his friends.

My deepest gratitude goes to my parents, who supported me along my journey on every step of the way. I am very thankful to my girlfriend, who tolerated my long nights in front of this text and helped me to overcome doubts that I had when inspiration was nowhere to be found. Many thanks to my sister, who gave me endless support throughout this process. Special thanks for close collaboration and great friendship goes to my great friend and colleague Miloš Radovanović, along with our colleague Gabriele Giganti, who shared his wisdom and good sense of humor when it was much needed.

About the Reviewer

Laurent Janolin is the founder and Associate Director of Live Session.
Web enthusiast, he loves working on how technology can help professionals to
develop their competencies, get things done, and improve their business. With Live
Session's team, Laurent helps companies to successfully deploy more than 1,000
webinars and virtual training classrooms per year in the banking, pharmaceutical,
and training industries.

To know more about Live Session, go to `http://www.live-session.eu`. To get in
touch with Laurent, send an e-mail to `laurent.janolin@live-session.fr`.

www.PacktPub.com

Support files, eBooks, discount offers and more

You might want to visit www.PacktPub.com for support files and downloads related to your book.

Did you know that Packt offers eBook versions of every book published, with PDF and ePub files available? You can upgrade to the eBook version at www.PacktPub.com and as a print book customer, you are entitled to a discount on the eBook copy. Get in touch with us at service@packtpub.com for more details.

At www.PacktPub.com, you can also read a collection of free technical articles, sign up for a range of free newsletters and receive exclusive discounts and offers on Packt books and eBooks.

http://PacktLib.PacktPub.com

Do you need instant solutions to your IT questions? PacktLib is Packt's online digital book library. Here, you can access, read and search across Packt's entire library of books.

Why Subscribe?

- Fully searchable across every book published by Packt
- Copy and paste, print and bookmark content
- On demand and accessible via web browser

Free Access for Packt account holders

If you have an account with Packt at www.PacktPub.com, you can use this to access PacktLib today and view nine entirely free books. Simply use your login credentials for immediate access.

Table of Contents

Preface

Modern world organizations require effective collaboration in order to improve productivity. Today we live in an era of companies that are spread across different continents, while there is an ever-increasing need to effectively share information in real time and to discuss a multitude of ideas, no matter where we are.

Conferencing tools enable users to increase their productivity and improve communication with their functionalities that include interactive experiences supported by multiple features. One of the most advanced conferencing tools and the market leader today is Adobe Connect. With its features that include audio and video, various sharing capabilities, meeting recordings, advanced users management, and file sharing and transferring, it is a great tool that will help you organize and present your content in the most efficient manner while capturing audience with rich and engaging presentations.

What this book covers

Chapter 1, Starting With Adobe Connect Application, will cover the basics of the Adobe Connect 9 application, after which you will be able to navigate through the application.

Chapter 2, Creating an Adobe Connect Meeting Room, will teach us how to create meeting room in the application, to manage meeting attendees, and to send invitations for meetings.

Chapter 3, Managing Adobe Connect Meeting Room, will explain how to edit various settings for existing meetings.

Chapter 4, Customizing the Viewing Experience, will provide guidelines on how to create meeting room templates and customize the Connect application.

Chapter 5, The Content Library, will discuss how to use the Content library features.

Chapter 6, Meeting Room Overview, will walk us through the meeting room features and its functionalities.

Chapter 7, Sharing Presentations, will walk us through the share pod and its basic functionalities.

Chapter 8, Using a Whiteboard Feature in the Meeting Room, will walk us through the whiteboard features.

Chapter 9, Using Screen Sharing, will walk us through the screen sharing options for the share pod. After reading this chapter you will be able to share your desktop, applications, and windows.

Chapter 10, Customizing Pod Display, will acquaint us with the pod menu description, pod preferences, and how to manage pods.

Chapter 11, Customizing and Saving Layouts, will provide guidelines on how to create and manage meeting room layouts.

Chapter 12, Recording Adobe Connect Meetings, will teach us how to record and manage meetings.

Chapter 13, Sharing Files, Polls, and Web Links, will provide guidelines on how to use File Share Pod, Poll Pod and Web Links Pod.

Chapter 14, Managing Text Messages and Questions, will walk us through the use of the Chat Pod, the Notes Pod, and the Q &A Pod.

Chapter 15, Using Audio and Video, will discuss how to use the audio and video conferencing features of Adobe Connect.

Chapter 16, Using Breakout Rooms, will explain how to use breakout rooms and their features.

Chapter 17, Integrating With Microsoft Outlook and Other Applications, is not present in the book but is available as a free download from the following link: `http://www.packtpub.com/sites/default/files/downloads/Integrating_With_Microsoft_Outlook_and_Other_Applications.pdf`. This will guide us on how to use the external Connect applications, such as Connect Outlook Add-in and Connect Add-in for Microsoft Lync.

Chapter 18, Creating and Managing Adobe Connect Events, is not present in the book but is available as a free download from the following link: `http://www.packtpub.com/sites/default/files/downloads/Creating_and_Managing_Adobe_Connect_Events.pdf`. This will explain how to create and manage events.

What you need for this book

You can register for a free Adobe Connect trial account, and in order to successfully use a meeting room, you must have an Internet connection, any modern browser (for example, Mozilla Firefox, Google Chrome, or Internet Explorer), and an installed version of Flash Player. Minimum requirements are Flash 10.1 for Adobe Connect 8 and 10.3 for Adobe Connect 9.

Who this book is for

This book is for users who would like to start utilizing the Adobe Connect application for web meetings, eLearning, and Webinars, and for those who are looking to learn Connect and get up to speed with using all the features that will help them to enable instant access to their web conferences from any mobile device or desktop, to improve collaboration while engaging meeting participants with great video experience and rich multimedia features. Readers of this book will be able to improve their web conferencing experiences by driving more efficient meetings and much better collaboration for all participants.

Conventions

In this book, you will find a number of styles of text that distinguish between different kinds of information. Here are some examples of these styles, and an explanation of their meaning.

Code words in text are shown as follows: "Depending on Connect settings, it might be the case that initially the Shared Meetings folder is only available to those users with Admin or Meeting Host role."

New terms and **important words** are shown in bold. Words that you see on the screen, in menus or dialog boxes for example, appear in the text like this: "On the right-hand side of the **Main Menu** bar, there is a **Search** text field for quick search functionality".

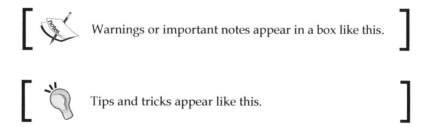

Warnings or important notes appear in a box like this.

Tips and tricks appear like this.

Reader feedback

Feedback from our readers is always welcome. Let us know what you think about this book—what you liked or may have disliked. Reader feedback is important for us to develop titles that you really get the most out of.

To send us general feedback, simply send an e-mail to feedback@packtpub.com, and mention the book title via the subject of your message.

If there is a topic that you have expertise in and you are interested in either writing or contributing to a book, see our author guide on www.packtpub.com/authors.

Customer support

Now that you are the proud owner of a Packt book, we have a number of things to help you to get the most from your purchase.

Errata

Although we have taken every care to ensure the accuracy of our content, mistakes do happen. If you find a mistake in one of our books—maybe a mistake in the text or the code—we would be grateful if you would report this to us. By doing so, you can save other readers from frustration and help us improve subsequent versions of this book. If you find any errata, please report them by visiting http://www.packtpub. com/submit-errata, selecting your book, clicking on the **errata submission form** link, and entering the details of your errata. Once your errata are verified, your submission will be accepted and the errata will be uploaded on our website, or added to any list of existing errata, under the Errata section of that title. Any existing errata can be viewed by selecting your title from http://www.packtpub.com/support.

Piracy

Piracy of copyright material on the Internet is an ongoing problem across all media. At Packt, we take the protection of our copyright and licenses very seriously. If you come across any illegal copies of our works, in any form, on the Internet, please provide us with the location address or website name immediately so that we can pursue a remedy.

Please contact us at `copyright@packtpub.com` with a link to the suspected pirated material.

We appreciate your help in protecting our authors, and our ability to bring you valuable content.

Questions

You can contact us at `questions@packtpub.com` if you are having a problem with any aspect of the book, and we will do our best to address it.

1
Starting with Adobe Connect Application

Adobe Connect is a flash-powered platform, and depending upon licensing and permissions within your organization, you can create web meetings, e-learning courses, and virtual classrooms and webinars. So we can say that Adobe Connect encompasses three major components:

- Adobe Connect meetings
- Adobe Connect trainings
- Adobe Connect events

In this chapter, you will learn the following:

- Basics of Connect meetings feature
- How to log in to the Connect application
- Connect home page user interface

In order to help run and manage those features, Content Management and Administration features are provided. Also, reporting is another key element of Adobe Connect.

The central topic of this book will be the Adobe Connect meeting feature. Of course, we will cover most of the Content Management feature, as well as some of Basic Event Management features.

In this chapter, you will learn the basics of the Adobe Connect application. After this chapter, you will be ready to enter the application and navigate through different pages of the Connect.

The basics of Connect meetings

Adobe Connect Meeting can be best described as an online live conference software for multiple users. It is a web-based application that you can use to run an online conference meeting. The meeting room interface is combined from various components and a number of display containers that are named pods. By using the pods functionalities, meeting room provides several features for multiple users who play the role of meeting attendees.

Users have the ability to chat, broadcast live video and audio, share files, share computer screens, or use other interactive functionalities while using the meeting room. You will learn how to use all of those functionalities in the later chapters of this book.

In addition to the predefined default layouts, you can customize your own meeting room according to your needs. This feature will be explained in detail in *Chapter 10, Customizing Pod Display.*

Every meeting room that is created in the application is assigned its own URL address, and it is available until you delete it. You can access your meeting by clicking on the assigned URL, and you can use the same URL address to enter created meeting rooms several times. In *Chapter 2, Creating an Adobe Connect Meeting Room* and *Chapter 3, Managing Adobe Connect Meeting Room,* you will learn how to create and manage your own meeting rooms.

Based upon your assigned role, you will have different capabilities in a meeting. In order to successfully use meeting rooms, you must have an Internet connection, any modern browser (for example, Mozilla Firefox, Google Chrome, or Internet Explorer), and an installed version of Flash Player. Minimum requirement is Flash 10.1 for AC8 and 10.3 for AC9.

Logging in to the Connect application

By entering the URL address of your Connect instance, you will be presented with the login screen. On this page, you will need to enter your credentials in the form of an e-mail address (usually your e-mail address or any other login information your administrator provided you with) and password provided to you by your system administrator for the specific instance of Adobe Connect. Please see the following screenshot for the example of an application login screen. Note that you will be able to customize this login page with your own logo. We will see this in the *Customizing Login Page, Central Page, and Meeting Appearance* section of *Chapter 4, Customizing the Viewing Experience.*

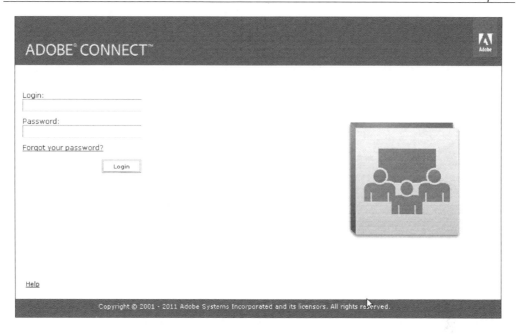

In addition to the fields provided for username and password on this page, you will find a link for password reset (**Forgot your password?**). This link can be used in case you forgot your password. In the bottom-left corner of the application, you will find the **Help** link that will redirect you to **Adobe Connect Help** page for detailed help of application functionalities. In case you enter incorrect credentials, the application will warn you and display an error message, **Invalid user name or password. Please try again**. Refer to the following screenshot:

In case you have forgotten your password, you can click on the **Forgot your password?** link, which will present you with the confirmation page for changing your password. Refer to the following screenshot:

The confirmation page will appear like the following screenshot:

Please enter your new password in the fields below and then press the "Submit New Password" button.

Passwords must conform to the following rules:
  • Passwords must be between 4 and 32 characters long.

New Password: [   ]

Confirm Password: [   ]

(Please note that passwords are case-sensitive.)

[Submit New Password]

The user interface of the Connect application

The user interface of the **Home** page can be divided into three areas:

  • **The Main Menu** area
  • **The Shortcut** area
  • **The Main** area

These areas are marked in the following screenshot:

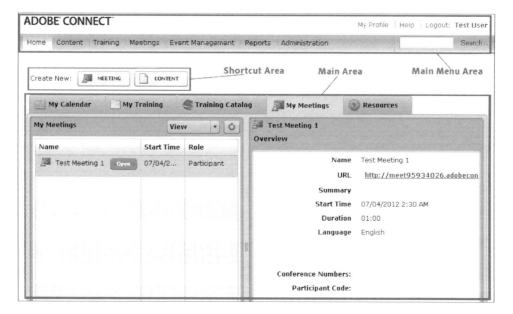

The Main Menu area

In the **Home** page of **Main Menu**, you will find several tabs that are used to navigate through the Adobe Connect application. Users can access each of these tabs based on their group membership privileges. There are tabs for the Content Management, Meeting Management, Event Management, Training Management, Reports, and Administration pages. Each of these pages is used to create, edit, and delete different Connect entities (meetings, trainings, contents, and events). Generally, group membership is defined by the system administrator.

If you try to access any tab for which you don't have permissions, the application will prompt you with a **Not Authorized** alert page.

If you are the administrator, either you did not log in as an administrator user, or you may want to check the users and groups in the **Administration** panel to make sure you're a member of the right group.

On the right-hand side of the **Main Menu** bar, there is a **Search** text field for quick search functionality. In addition to quick search, you will find the **Search** link. Based on the search parameters and optional filters, when you click on the **Go** button, the application will take you to the **Advance Search** page. The search functionality helps you to find any Connect entity (meeting, training, content, event, and so on) by using advanced criteria. Refer to the following screenshot:

In the upper-right corner, there are three additional links:

- **My Profile**: This link is used to display information about currently logged in users

- **Help**: This link will redirect you to the **Adobe Online Help** page

  Please note that this is different from the help you can access from the login page; this one is more like a user guide

- **Logout**: This link will log you out from the application

The Shortcut Menu area

In the **Shortcut** area, marked on the screenshot, in the beginning of this section, there are shortcuts that will help you to create meetings, content, or any other entity allowed in Connect. Shortcut buttons are enabled for creating entities based on the group membership privileges of the user that is currently logged in to the application. The screenshot shows an example of a user who is only part of the **Meeting Host** group. Based on his group membership, the application will display only shortcuts specific for creating meetings and contents.

The Main area

The **Main** area menu shown in the next screenshot provides you with information about all entities (meetings and trainings) that you are part of. On the left-hand side of this area is the list of all meetings in which you are participating.

Here you can view your role in all the listed meetings and the start time of the meeting. Next to the meeting name, there is an **Open** button that is used to quick launch the selected meeting.

On the right-hand side of the **Main** area, you will find detailed information for the selected meeting. You can also access a specific meeting by clicking on the URL address of the selected meeting.

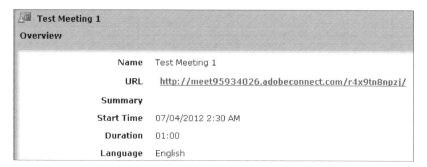

By clicking on the **My Calendar** tab, you will be presented with the calendar view for all events that you are participating in as shown in the following screenshot:

Summary

In this chapter, we have gone through some basic information regarding Adobe Connect. Now you know how to log in to Connect and how to navigate through the user interface of the application. We also talked about the **Home** page, and have described most of the functionalities that this page provides. Now you are able to go to the **Meeting Creation** page using **Main Menu** or using the shortcut button for creating meetings. In the next chapter, we will go through the meeting-creation process.

2
Creating an Adobe Connect Meeting Room

This chapter will demonstrate to the user how to successfully create a meeting room in the Adobe Connect application. By the end of this chapter, the user will be able to create a meeting room, manage meeting attendees, and create and send invitations in the Adobe Connect application.

In this chapter, you will learn the following:

- Meeting room roles
- The **Meeting Management** page
- The **Enter Meeting Information** page
- The **Participants Selection** page
- The **Send Invitations** page

Meeting room roles

Before we explain how to create a meeting room, we should familiarize ourselves with user roles that exist inside the meeting room. Users inside the meeting room are divided into four roles:

- **Host**: This is the role with maximum permissions in the meeting room role hierarchy. Users assigned with the host role can create meetings, invite participants, share content, and create templates and layouts. In addition to the listed capabilities, the host can change participants' roles, give enhanced rights to participants on certain pods, move other users to breakout rooms, start audio conference, stop audio conferences, use prepare mode, use presenter mode, and record a meeting.

- **Presenter**: This is the role next to the host in the role hierarchy. Users with presenter rights can share their screen, meeting content or content that is already loaded inside Content Library, as well as their presentations or image files. These users can use presenter and prepare mode as well. On the other hand, promoting or devoting other users, moving other users to breakout rooms, and creating layouts are some of the options that are not available to the presenter role.

- **Participants**: These are registered Connect users who join specific meetings. They can watch what are the users with presenter or host privileges sharing, use the chat pod, and mute and un-mute speakers on their computers. If participants join an audio conference, they will hear the audio broadcast as well.

- **Guest**: There is no difference between participants and guest role when users already join a meeting. Guests will have exactly the same privileges and features available as participants. The main difference is that the guest users can join a meeting room only by entering their alias names while they are joining the meeting.

Depending on your role, certain icons will be associated with your name in the attendees pod.

You don't have to worry because you're not completely familiar with features tied to different roles that we mentioned earlier. We will explain them in detail in further chapters of this book.

The Meeting Management page

In the previous chapter, we demonstrated how to log in to the Adobe Connect application. When you click on the **Meetings** tab in the main menu navigation bar of the application, you will be presented with the **Meeting Management** page.

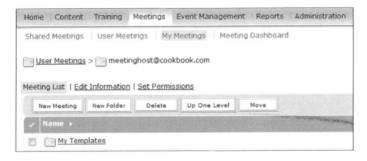

On the **Meeting Management** page, you will find several options that will help you to create wanted meetings. When selected, the **Meetings** tab will display an additional navigation bar, where you will be provided with links for the following options:

- **Shared Meetings**
- **User Meetings**
- **My Meetings**
- **Meeting Dashboard**

Shared Meeting

When you click on the **Shared Meetings** item link, you will be able to see the list of all the meetings that are shared with you. Shared meetings are those meetings that can be created by registered Connect users. By registered users, we mean users who can log in to the Connect application with its assigned login credentials. The shared meetings list will display information about your meetings that you created, as well as shared meetings that are created by other registered users. In the shared meeting list, users will also find the shared templates. Templates are very useful since they help to create new meetings with standard layouts (one for training, one for project management, one for a specific customer meeting, and so on) without the risk that other users will change the layout (*Chapter 4, Customizing the Viewing Experience* will give you more info regarding templates). Refer to the following screenshot:

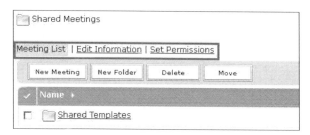

In the upper section (except already explained), in selected **Meeting List**, you will additionally find two very useful links: **Edit Information** and **Set Permissions**. By using these links, it is possible to rename the folder, add a detailed description, or change the access rights for this folder (for example, you can grant other users the ability to see what is in this folder). Depending on the Connect settings, it might be the case that initially the `Shared Meetings` folder is only available to those users with Admin or Meeting Host role.

User Meetings

By clicking on the **User Meetings** link, logged in users with administrative privileges have the ability to see a list of folders that belong to all users in the Adobe Connect application, as shown in the following screenshot:

When an administrator clicks on any of the listed folders, another page is opened. This page contains links to all personal meetings previously created by the selected user.

When any of the provided links for meetings are selected, the **Meeting Information** page for the selected meeting will be displayed. The **Meeting Information** page contains the **Enter Meeting Room** button that enables users to join a preferred meeting conference.

Users who do not have administrative privileges cannot access the **User Meetings** page.

If they attempt to access the page, they will be prompted with the message, **Not Authorized. You do not have permission to access this item**.

My Meetings

When you click on the **My Meetings** link, a new page is opened. This page will display all meetings for which you are in the Meeting Host role. You can see the detailed meeting information page or enter any of the provided meeting rooms by selecting displayed links for these functionalities.

Meeting Dashboard

By selecting the **Meeting Dashboard** link, users are offered reports that provide detailed information about certain Adobe Connect Meeting categories. Generally, there are three reports available on this page:

- **Most Active Meetings Over Last 30 Days**
- **Most Participant Meetings Over Last 30 Days**
- **Most Viewed Recordings over Last 30 Days**

When users create meetings, they can be associated with either My Meetings or Shared Meetings group. In the bottom part of the **Meeting Management** page, you will find five buttons displayed:

- **New Meeting**
- **New Folder**
- **Delete**
- **Up One Level**
- **Move**

We will describe the **Move** button functionality in more detail in *Chapter 4, Customizing the Viewing Experience.*

The **Delete** button is used when users need to delete a particular meeting. In order to delete any meeting, the user needs to select specific meetings by clicking on the checkbox to the left-hand side of the meeting name. Once when the meeting is selected, click on the **Delete** button to permanently remove the meeting from the application, as shown in the following screenshot:

The **New Folder** button is used to create a new folder inside the meeting list. Users can create as many folders as they need in order to organize meetings according to their logical needs. For example, you can create two folders with names `Private` and `Business`, and later on when you learn how to create meetings, you can add them in these newly created folders.

The **Up One Level** button will take the user back to the previous menu item.

Now we can discuss our main topic of interest for this chapter and that is the **New Meeting** button. By clicking on this button, you will start the **Meeting Creation** wizard. Once you start the wizard, the **Enter Meeting Information** page will open.

The Enter Meeting Information page

The **Meeting Creation** wizard consists of three pages. The first page of the wizard is the **Enter Meeting Information** page. This page consists of two sections; the upper section of the page is titled **Meeting Information**, and the lower section is titled **Audio Conference Settings**. The **Audio Conference Settings** section is optional, and we will skip this part until Chapter 15, where we will write about using audio and video in Adobe Connect. At the bottom of the **Enter Meeting Information** page, you will find the **Cancel**, **Previous**, **Next**, and **Finish** buttons.

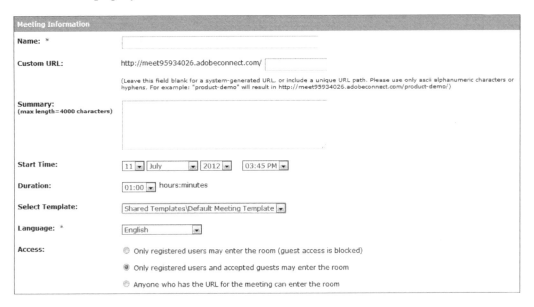

The Meeting Information section

In the **Meeting Information** section, the user should enter details about the meeting that is going to be created. Please note that the red asterisk indicates the required mandatory fields as shown in the previous screenshot. Two fields that are mandatory for meeting creation are **Language** and **Name**. Out of those two fields, the **English** language is selected as a default language in the **Language** drop-down list. The user will have to fill out only one mandatory field on this form, so it makes it very easy to create a new meeting. To summarize things, in order to create a new meeting at a very low level, the user will need to execute the next three operations:

1. Hit the **New Meeting** button.
2. Type in the name of the meeting.
3. Hit the **Finish** button at the bottom of the page.

Beside these mandatory fields, the user can include more info while creating a meeting. In order to do so, the user will need to fill the following optional data:

- **Custom URL**: As a meeting host, we recommend that you fill out the **Custom URL** text field, so you will be able to track down your meetings easier, and it will also be much more easier for your participants to type in your meeting URL, if needed. If you do so, the URL for the meeting might look like http://meet95934026.adobeconnect.com/CookBook. Otherwise, once when you click on the **Finish** button, the application will autogenerate your meeting URL, which will result in a URL similar to `http://meet95934026.adobeconnect.com/r37y6n43npi`.

  Be careful about how you create a meeting since the URL is the only field that cannot be modified once a meeting is created. You can change the date, the description, even the title of the meeting but not the URL. So, for example, if you misspell the custom URL field, you'll have to delete it and create your meeting again.

- **Summary**: Here, the user can enter comments (limited to 4,000 characters). Information entered in this field is sent in the e-mail invitation for the meeting.

- **Start Time**: Use this field when you want to specify the start time of a meeting. Here, you can define the date, month, year, and exact start time of the meeting.

- **Duration**: This field is used in order to enter the planned duration time for the meeting by entering values for hours and minutes.

- **Select Template**: You can select a template for the meeting from the drop-down list. For the purpose of this chapter, we will pick the **Default** meeting template, since in *Chapter 4*, *Customizing the Viewing Experience*, we will give you a detailed explanation on templates.

- **Access**: This field offers three radio button options that the user can select:

  - **Only registered users may enter the room** (guest access is blocked): By selecting this option once when user enters the meeting URL in any browser, the login page will appear. The only way to join the meeting will be to enter the username and password in the appropriate fields on the login page. The meeting host will need to accept the incoming users.

- ○ **Only registered users and accepted guests may enter the room**: In case this option is selected once when login page is displayed, the user will have to select an option whether to join a meeting as a registered user by entering the username and password or as a guest. To join a meeting as a guest, select the **Enter as a Guest** radio button option. The only additional info that needs to be provided is the guest user's name that will be displayed in the attendees pod. The meeting host will also need to accept the incoming users.

- ○ **Anyone who has the URL for the meeting can enter the room**: This option enables users to join a meeting as a guest or registered user, but in difference to the previous option, they will automatically join a meeting without the need for hosts to accept them.

Important notice here is that all these non-mandatory fields are only designed to share info with the participants and to get organized better within Connect. However, they have no impact on when one can open a meeting room. For instance, setting up the date field on January 7, 2013 will not block the user from opening a meeting room on January 8, 2013. Also, the host can change access behavior within a meeting room itself. This option can be useful, if, for example, you have originally blocked guest access and you need a participant who does not have an account on your platform to join a meeting. A detailed explanation on how this can be done from within a meeting is explained in *Chapter 6, Meeting Room Overview*.

In order to access the second page of the **Meeting Creation** wizard, the user needs to click on the **Next** button. Once you click on the **Next** button, the **Select Participants** page will be loaded.

The Select Participants page

This page is the second step in creating a meeting with the help of the **Meeting Creation** wizard. Refer to the following screenshot:

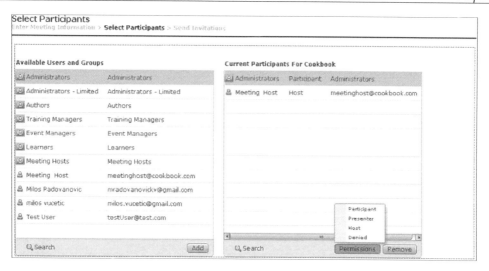

On the left-hand side of the window, you will find different users and groups that can be added by default as participants in a meeting. If you include a particular group, all users registered within that group in the Connect application will be able to join the meeting by entering the meeting URL and login credentials. If you decide to select a specific user listed in the **Available Users** and **Groups** list on the left-hand side of the window, you will grant meeting access rights only for the selected user.

Now that you are familiar with the process of including meeting participants, you can manage participant roles in the meeting room. We will demonstrate two examples that will explain how to include all administrators as meeting participants and how to include a specific user as a presenter in a meeting.

Example 1 – granting administrators group participant permission

Follow the given steps:

1. Click on the **Administrators** group in the **Available Users** and **Groups** table on the left-hand side.

2. Click on the **Add** button.

3. The **Administrators** group will now be shown in the **Current Participants for Cookbook** table on the right-hand side of the window. By examining the list of participants, you can verify that all members of the **Administrators** group will be granted with participant permission.

Example 2 – granting presenter permission to a specific user

Follow the given steps:

1. Click on any username in the **Available Users** and **Groups** table on the left-hand side.

2. Click on the **Add** button.

3. The user will now be shown in the **Current Participants for Cookbook** table on the right-hand side of the window with participant permission.

4. Select the same user in the **Current Participants for Cookbook** table on the right-hand side of the window.

5. Click on the **Permission** button.

6. Select the **Presenter** option from the menu.

7. Note that the user in the **Current Participants for Cookbook** table on the right-hand side is now granted with presenter permission.

After explaining how to include different users and manage their roles in your meeting, we can proceed with the third and final step for meeting creation by using the **Meeting Creation** wizard.

The Send Invitations page

Features implemented on this page allow you to send e-mail invitations to your meeting invitees. On this page, you can find different options that allow modifications of your e-mail notification.

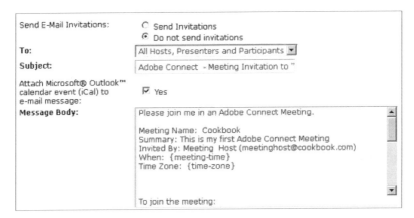

The user interface of the Send Invitations page

The **Send E-Mail Invitations** radio button defines whether you want to send invitations or not. We will mention here that by default the **Do Not Send Invitations** option is active, so there is no risk that you will send an invitation if you do not want to. If you select the **Send Invitations** option, you have to select recipients from the drop-down list next to **To: label**. The following are the options for the recipients list:

- **All hosts, Presenters and Participants**
- **Host only**
- **Presenters only**
- **Participants only**

By selecting any of the defined groups, the users belonging to these groups will receive e-mail invitations. Under the previous radio button, there is a **Subject:** text field. You can enter any text here, which will be used as an e-mail subject when the meeting invitation is sent.

Click on the **iCal** checkbox in case you want to include the Microsoft Outlook calendar appointment. In the **Message Body** comment box section, the application will generate detailed meeting information for recipients. The **Message Body** box contains the meeting name, dedicated meeting URL, start time, end time, and customized description of the meeting in the summary part of the **Message Body** box.

By completing this page, we reviewed all of the features that are implemented on the **Send Invitation** page and all of the pages of the **Meeting Creation** wizard. The only thing that is left over now is to click on the **Finish** button in order to create a meeting. After clicking on the **Finish** button, you will be redirected to the **Meeting Information** page. On this page, you can click on the meeting URL or on the **Enter Meeting Room** button in order to join the meeting.

By now, your default meeting room will appear as shown in the following screenshot:

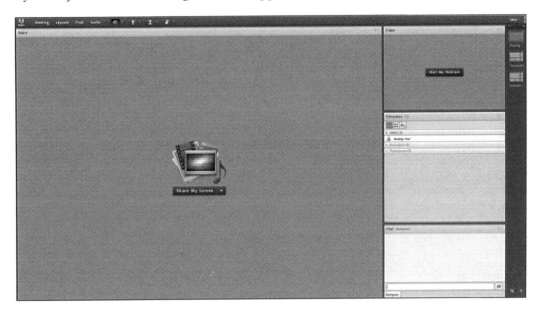

Congratulations! You have successfully created and joined your first Adobe Connect meeting room.

Summary

In this chapter, we have gone through the description of a **Meeting Management** page, **Enter Meeting Information** page, and information on how to manage meeting participants. Now you will be able to create a meeting room in the Adobe Connect application, manage your meeting participants, and send e-mail invitations to them. The next chapter will give you a detailed description of the **Meeting Information** page and teach you how to update and edit the meeting info.

3

Managing Adobe Connect Meeting Room

In the previous chapter, you learned how to create and join the Adobe Connect meeting. In addition to the information provided in the previous chapters, by the end of this chapter, you will master all functionalities on how to edit different settings for already existing meetings.

In this chapter we will cover the following topics:

- The **Meeting information** page
- The **Managing Edit information** page
- The **Managing Edit participants** page
- The **Managing Invitations** page
- The **Managing Uploaded content** page
- The **Managing Reports** page
- The **Managing Recordings** page

The Meeting Information page

At the very end of the previous chapter, we mentioned the existence of the **Meeting Information** page. In order to get to this page, you will first need to navigate to the **Meeting List** page by following these steps:

1. Log in to the Connect application.
2. Click on the **Meetings** tab in the **Home Page** main menu.

When you access the **Meetings** page, the **My Meetings** link is opened by default and a view is set on the **Meeting List** tab. You will find the meeting created in the previous chapter that is listed on this page as shown in the following screenshot:

By clicking on the **Cookbook Meeting** option in the **Name** column (marked with a red outline), you will be presented with the **Meeting Information** page. In the section titled **Meeting Information**, you can examine various pieces of information about the selected meeting. On this page, you can review **Name**, **Summary**, **Start Time**, **Duration**, **Number of users in room** (that are currently present in the meeting room), **URL**, **Language** (selected), and the **Access** rights of the meeting.

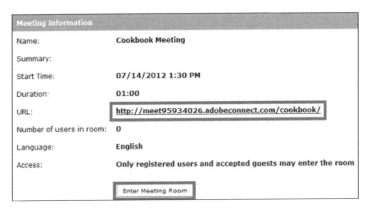

The two most important fields are marked with a red outline in the previous screenshot. The first one is the link to the meeting URL and the second is the **Enter Meeting Room** button. You can join the selected meeting room by clicking on any of these two options.

In the upper portion of this page, you will notice the navigation bar with the following links:

- **Meeting Information**
- **Edit Information**
- **Edit Participants**

- **Invitations**
- **Uploaded Content**
- **Recordings**
- **Reports**

By selecting any of these links, you will open pages associated with them. Our main focus of this chapter will be on the functionalities of these pages. Since we have explained the **Meeting Information** page, we can proceed to the **Edit Information** page.

The Edit Information page

The **Edit Information** page is very similar to the **Enter Meeting Information** page. We will briefly inform you about the meeting settings, which you can edit on this page. These settings are:

- **Name**
- **Summary**
- **Start time**
- **Duration**
- **Language**
- **Access**
- **Audio conference settings**

Any changes made on this page are preserved by clicking on the **Save** button that you will find at very bottom of this page. Changes will not affect participants who are already logged in to the room, except changes to the **Audio Conference** settings. Next to the **Save** button, you will find the **Cancel** button. Any changes made on the **Edit Information** page, which are not already saved will be reverted by clicking on the **Cancel** button.

The Edit Participants page

After the **Edit Information** page, it's time for us to access the next page by clicking on the **Edit Participants** link in the navigation bar. This link will take you to the **Select Participants** page that we've already described in the previous chapter. In addition to the already described features, we will introduce you to a couple more functionalities that will help you to add participants, change their roles, or remove them from the meeting.

Example 1 – changing roles

In this example, we will change the role of the administrators group from participant to presenter by using the **Search** button. This feature is of great help when there are a large number of Connect users that are already added as meeting participants. In order to do so, you will need to follow the steps listed:

1. In the **Current Participants For Cookbook Meeting** table on the right-hand side, click on the **Search** button located in the lower-left corner of the table. When you click on the **Search** button, a text field for instant search will be displayed.

2. In the text field, enter the name of the **Administrators** group or part of the group name (the auto-complete function should recognize the name of the present group).

3. When the group is present in the table, select it.

4. Click on the **Set User Role** button.

5. Select new role for this group in the menu. For the purpose of this example, we will select the **Presenter** role.

6. By completing this action, you will grant **Presenter** privileges in the **Cookbook Meeting** table to all the administrators as shown in the following screenshot:

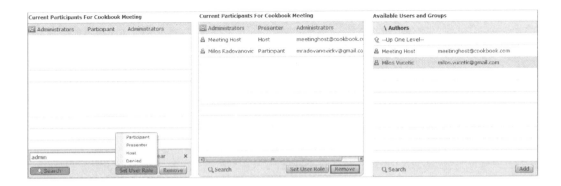

Example 2 – removing a user

In this example, we will show you how to remove a specific user from the selected meeting. For the purpose of this exercise, we will remove the **Administrators** group from the **Participants** list. In order to complete this action, please follow the given steps:

1. Select **Administrators** in the **Current Participants For Cookbook Meeting** table.

2. Click on the **Remove** button.

3. Now, all the members of this group will be excluded from the meeting, and **Administrators** should not be present in the list.

Example 3 – adding a specific user

This example will demonstrate how to add a specific user from any group. For example, we will add a user from the **Authors** group to the **Current Participants** list.

1. In the **Available users and Groups** table, double-click on the **Authors** group.

   This action will change the user interface of this table and list all the users that belong to the **Authors** group. Please note that table header is now changed to **Authors**.

2. Select a specific user and click on the **Add** button.

3. This will add the selected user from the **Authors** group to the **Current Participants For Cookbook Meeting** table.

One thing that we would like to mention here is the ability to perform multiple selections in both the **Available Users and Groups** and **Current Participants For Cookbook Meeting** tables. To enable multiple selection functionality, select a specific user and group by clicking and selecting *Ctrl* and *Shift* on the keyboard at the same time. By demonstrating these examples, we reviewed the **Edit Participant link** functionalities.

The Meeting Invitations page

By selecting the **Invitations** link, you will be redirected to the **Invitations** page. This page will provide you with features that will help you to send invitations to your meeting attendees. The **Invitations** page includes meeting summary, start date, duration, and meeting URL. This page is very similar to the **Send Invitations** page, except for the radio button for sending invitations that are not displayed.

We will present you with two scenarios to manage invitations:

- The first one is if you are on the **Edit Information** page. If the **Only registered users may enter the room** option (guest access is blocked) or the **Only registered users and accepted guests may enter the room** option is selected, you can choose to send an invitation among the groups, such as **All Hosts, Presenters and Participants, Hosts Only, Presenters Only**, and **Participants Only**.

- The second scenario is if you are on the **Edit Information** page. If the **Anyone who has the URL for the meeting can enter the room** option is selected, then you can perform the following actions on the **Invitations** page:

  i. Click on the **Send Email** button to receive an e-mail with your user ID. Later on you can forward this e-mail from any e-mail client or from webmail to any contact from your contacts list.

  ii. Copy the content of the message body and send it to your contacts by using any e-mail client.

In addition to selecting the people we want to send notifications to, we can edit the e-mail subject and message body on this page. If you would like to attach the Outlook calendar event to the e-mail, select the checkbox next to the **Attach Microsoft Outlook calendar event (iCal) to email message** label. Otherwise, keep this checkbox unchecked.

The Uploaded Content page

In order to navigate to this page, you can click on the **Uploaded Content** link in the navigation menu. In order to better explain the functionalities on the **Uploaded Content** page, we already set up a meeting room for cookbook meeting and shared the content inside the meeting room. We will go into more details and describe how this should be done in *Chapter 9, Using Screen Sharing*. In the table displayed on the **Uploaded Content** page, you can find a list of all content that has been previously shared. If you have not opened your meeting room yet, this list will be empty. Refer to the following screenshot:

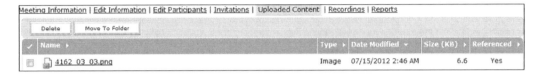

Each type of content listed in this table is described with these parameters:

- **Name**
- **Type**
- **Date Modified**
- **Size (KB)**
- **Referenced** (this determines whether the content is still in use in the meeting room)

If you want to edit content settings or review content, click on the desired data listed in the content list. When you select content from the list, the **Uploaded Content Information** tab opens. In addition to the functionality for editing content information, you will also find the URL for the selected content. By clicking on this link, you will see the content of the sample image listed in the example of the **Meeting Information** page.

Let's go back to the **Uploaded Content** page. In order to return to this page, click on the **Return To Uploaded Content** link. You can also click on the back arrow in your browser. In order to remove content from the **Uploaded Content** table, perform the following:

1. Click on the checkbox on the left-hand side of content name.
2. Click on the **Delete** button.

In addition to the **Delete** button, you will also find the **Move** to **Folder** button on this page. This button can be used to move selected content to `Content Library`. Depending on the user's permissions in the **Content Library** folder, the uploaded content can be moved to the `Shared Content`, `User Content`, or `My Content` folder. In order to move the content, you can follow the given steps:

1. Click on the checkbox next to one or more pieces of content you would like to move.

2. Click on the **Move** to **Folder** button; the **Folder** page will appear.

3. Select the `My Content` folder on this page.

4. Click on the **Move** button.

5. After doing so, you will be prompted with the message, **The following items were moved successfully**.

By completing these steps, we have reviewed all the functionalities of the **Uploaded Content** page. Now, we can proceed to the next item.

The Meeting Recordings page

For the time being, we will skip further explanation of the **Recordings** link in the navigation menu since *Chapter 12, Recording Adobe Connect Meetings*, will be dedicated to explaining ways to create and manage meeting recordings.

The Meeting Reports page

In order to get to the **Meeting Reports** page, you can click on the **Meeting Reports** link in the navigation menu. This page contains reports of the selected meeting. These reports are divided into four categories:

- **By Attendees**: This report lets you see the name and e-mail address of any meeting participant. Additional information provided by this report is the time when users joined or left the meeting. The following screenshot will describe the filter creation and report the download process:

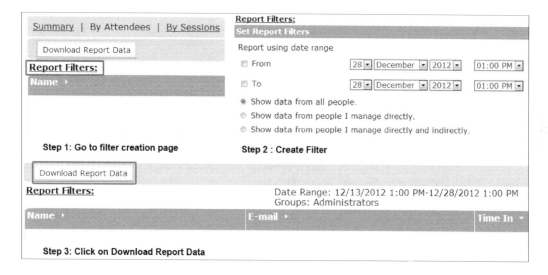

- **By Sessions**: These reports show the start and end time of each meeting session, together with the number of attendees per session. By clicking on the session number, you will see the complete list of meeting participants with their names, meeting entry, and exit times.

    Both of these reports have a button that will let you download the report data. They also contain the **Report Filters** link that will open the **Report Filters** page. On this page, you can select different settings for a specific report. You can customize the date range, add and remove certain groups from the report, and select the checkbox to show the data from people you manage directly or indirectly.

- **By Questions**: This report shows a list of polls by number, session number, and question. In the **Reports** column, the user can choose between **View answer distribution** and **View user responses**. The first option displays a pie chart, where each offered voting option in the poll is shown by a different color. The second option displays poll question along with offered answers followed by the complete list of users who took part in voting, along with their vote results.

- **Summary**: This report type shows the most common meeting information: name, URL, most recent session start time, and the highest number of participants who joined the meeting room at any given time.

Summary

By now, you should have enough knowledge about managing functionalities of Connect meetings, so you should be able to edit already existing meetings to satisfy your needs.

4

Customizing the Viewing Experience

At this point, you should be familiar with managing Adobe Connect meeting rooms along with all their managing functionalities. We will continue with customizing the viewing experience. This chapter will teach you how to create meeting room templates, as well as how to customize the Connect application through various recipes.

In this chapter we will show you the following features of Adobe Connect:

- Meeting room templates
- Description of information preserved in a template
- Creating a meeting room template
- Converting a meeting room into a template
- Applying a template to a new meeting
- Customizing the login page, central page, and meeting appearance

Meeting room templates

What is a template for a meeting room? A meeting room template is a meeting with predefined settings. Meeting settings that can be predefined are meeting configurations, meeting content, and meeting layouts, and the way they are presented to the user. As far as meetings are concerned, there is one built-in template that exists in Connect as a **default meeting template**. In addition to the default meeting template, there are two additional built-in templates, namely, a template for trainings and a template for events. The purpose of a template is to help you to quickly create a meeting without a need for additional customized settings each time you need to create a meeting.

When creating a new meeting, you have the option to use the default template as well as to use customized templates that you previously created. In our first example, we will first create a new meeting by using the default meeting template, and in our next example, we will create a meeting with our own custom template.

After you have successfully logged in to the **Home** page, in order to create a new meeting, you will need to navigate to the **Enter meeting information** page. This could be done in two ways: you can click on the **Meetings** tab in the main menu or on the **Meeting** button as shown in the following screenshot:

For the purpose of this chapter, the most important part of the **Enter meeting information** page is the **Select Template** drop-down list. Here, you can choose the desired template from a list of provided templates. For now, the only available template is **Default Meeting Template**, and it will be automatically selected.

On this page, you will be prompted to fill in the meeting information as described in the previous chapters. In the **Name** field, enter Cookbook Meeting as the meeting name. We will use this meeting as an example for further explanations of functionalities in this chapter. When you click on the **Finish** button in the lower part of the page, your sample meeting room will be created successfully.

Meeting room content, as shown in the following screenshots, will be present when we create a meeting from a default template.

Most common configurations when creating a new meeting from default templates are:

- Only registered users and accepted guests may enter the room in the **Meeting Information** section

- Do not include any audio conference with this meeting in the **Audio Conference Settings** section

- A meeting room created in this manner will contain three layouts, namely, sharing layout, collaboration layout, and discussion layout

- ○ Sharing layout is customized so that share options can be easily accessed
- ○ Discussion layout is optimized for users with a need for frequent use of conversation pods, such as chat and note pod
- ○ Collaboration layout is created for users who need to annotate some information on content and to use a whiteboard during a meeting

Now, when you are familiar with the default template and the template purpose, we can continue with the next step, which is the creation of your own template and its application on new meetings. Before we go on with template creation, you will learn what kind of information is preserved in a template.

Information preserved in a template

A template is simply a duplicate of an original meeting. Some settings in a template are saved by default and some aren't.

Settings that are saved in a template are:

- **Meeting Room background customization**
- **Pods with their name, size and position**
- **Layouts**
- **Notes in the note pod**
- **Polls in the poll pod**
- **Questions and Answers in the Q&A pod**
- **Whiteboard content**
- **Links in the Web Link pod**
- **Message which is displayed to other users when meeting ends**

On the other side, settings that are not saved are:

- **Chat pod messages**
- **Audio settings**
- **Audio setup wizard settings**

Now that we have listed the information that is preserved in a template, we will continue with the next step.

Creating a meeting room template

In this section, we will show you how to customize meeting room appearance and how to use this appearance in a meeting room as a default template while creating new meetings. In order to demonstrate this, we will start a new meeting and create a new layout, which will be customized for our needs. In order to create a new empty layout, please follow the given steps:

1. Click on the **Layouts** link in the meeting room main menu.
2. In the **Layout** menu, click on the **Create New Layout...** option.
3. When the **Create a New Layout** dialog appears, the **Create a new blank layout** option is selected. All we need to do here is to enter the layout name and click on the **OK** button.

Now it's time to give a new look to our meeting room. We will do this by including different kinds of pods in the previously created layout. For this example, we will choose web links, notes, and share pod for the new layout look. In order to do this, follow the given steps:

1. Click on the **Pods** link in the meeting room main menu.
2. In the **Pods** menu, choose the desired pod. We will select **Share**, **Notes**, and **Web Links** pods.
3. Depending on the choice of the selected pod in the **Pods** menu, the submenu will contain options such as **Share**, **Notes**, or **Add New Web Links**.

After we complete these steps, the appearance of a meeting room might be like the one shown in the following screenshot:

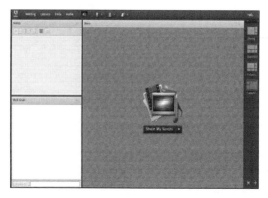

Customized layout

We used the word "might" since the position and size of the pods can be arranged simply by resizing them or moving them to a different position with the drag-and-drop functionality.

Before we close this meeting room, simply add a note in a note pod.

You can close this meeting room for now, because you will need to go back to the Connect application. As we mentioned previously, please remember the name of the meeting you have created, so you can go back to it. In this chapter, we used **Cookbook Meeting**.

Converting a meeting room into a template

Now that you've created a template for the meeting room appearance, you will learn to convert a meeting to a template. In order to do so, you will need to go back to the **Meetings** page in a Connect application as described earlier. You will notice your meeting (**Cookbook Meeting**) in the **Meetings List** window. Select the meeting by clicking on the checkbox next to the meeting name, and then click on the **Move** button, as shown in the following screenshot:

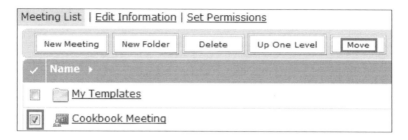

After you click on the button, you will see the **Move** page.

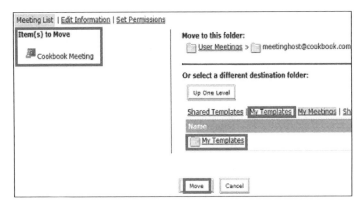

Move page view

On the left-hand side of the **Move** page, you can see that your selected meeting is shown in the **Item(s) to Move** section. In our example, only **Cookbook Meeting** is displayed. In order to convert the meeting room into a template, you can follow these steps:

1. On the right-hand side of the **Move** page, click on the **My Templates** tab or `My Templates` folder (marked with red outline in the previous screenshot).

2. Click on the **Move** button (marked with a red outline in the previous screenshot).

After completing these steps, you will successfully move the selected meeting into the `My Templates` folder. As a confirmation of the move action, you will see the message shown in the following screenshot:

In case you decide to move this meeting into the `Shared Templates` folder, you should know that by doing this, newly created templates will be available to all users who can create a meeting.

By completing these steps, conversion of a meeting room into a template is done.

Applying a template to a new meeting

Since you have moved a meeting to the My Templates folder, you should now get familiar with how to use newly created templates when creating new meetings. In order to do so, you can start creating a meeting creation from the **New Meeting** button shortcut on the **Home** page. Another way to complete this action is by clicking on the **Meetings** link in the main menu of the Adobe Connect **Home** page followed by clicking on the **New Meeting** button on the **Meeting List** page. You will be directed to the **Enter Meeting Information** page. You can select your template from the **Select Template** drop-down list and select the **My Templates/Cookbook Meeting** option.

Select Template:	Shared Templates\Default Meeting Template ▾
	Shared Templates\Default Event Template
Language: *	Shared Templates\Default Meeting Template
	Shared Templates\Default Training Template
	My Templates\Cookbook Meeting

After selecting your template, enter a meeting name and click on the **Finish** button. After clicking on the button, the **Meeting Information** page will load. You can click on the **Enter Meeting Room** button, and you will join a new Connect meeting. The meeting room should look exactly like the one shown in the **Customized Layout** and **Meeting Room** appearance screenshots, and all meeting template information should be preserved; you can verify the existence of the note previously added in the notes pod in our case.

We are finished with explanation on how to create templates for meeting rooms, and in the next part of this chapter we will focus on customizing the Adobe Connect application.

Customizing the login page, central page, and meeting appearance

Adobe Connect provides features for meeting room customization along with features for login page and central page customization. These features are only available to users with administrator privileges in the system. We recommend that you log in to the Connect application with the administrator role account in order to follow instructions for this part of the chapter. In order to get to the **Customization** page, you will need to complete the following steps:

1. Click on the **Administration** tab of the **Home** page in the main menu.

2. Select the **Customization** tab in the administration submenu.

You will notice that you are on the **Customization** page now. This page consists of three buttons and three tabs. The following is the list of buttons and their functions:

- **Clear**: This button cancels changes
- **Apply**: By clicking on this button, you will confirm the changes that you created
- **Reset to default**: Clicking on this button will set your default view to the login page

Now, we will list tabs on the **Customize** page:

- **Customize Central**
- **Customize Login**
- **Customize Meeting**

How to customize the central page

For customization of the Connect **Home** page, click on the **Customize Central** tab.

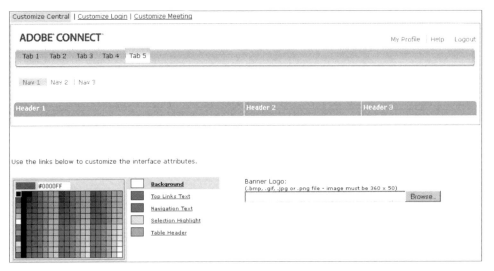

Customize Central tab

The interface customization options that are offered for the **Customize Central** page are:

- **Background**
- **Top Links Text**
- **Navigation Text**
- **Selection Highlights**
- **Table Header**

For any of these options, you can change the color by selecting the desired option and then selecting the required color from the color picker next to the option's links. You can also choose your page color by entering an HTML color code in the text field above color picker (for example, #0000FF). In addition to color changes that you can apply, you can also modify the **Banner Logo**. The **Banner Logo** image can be changed by clicking on the **Browse** button and by selecting the appropriate image file from your computer. Image size for the **Banner Logo** image should be **360 x 50** pixels. All changes that are created should be saved by clicking on the **Apply** button. If you reopen the **Customize Central** page, you should be able to see all the changes that you have applied to this page. If the changes are not visible immediately, refreshing the browser or clearing the browser cache should help.

How to customize the login page

In order to customize the login page, click on the **Customize Login** tab.

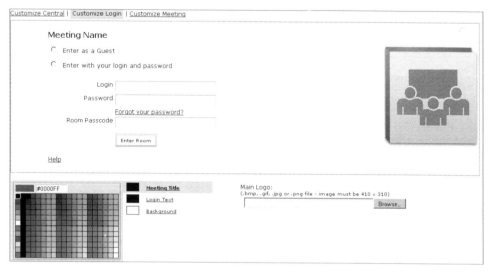

Customize Login tab

In the bottom-left corner of this tab, you can choose the changes you would like to apply. Changes options that are available are:

- **Meeting Title**
- **Login Text**
- **Background**

In order to change the background color, for example, you will need to select the **Background** option, and then select the preferred color from the color picker next to the options links. You can also choose your background color by entering the HTML color code in the text field above color picker (for example, #0000FF). After you select your choices, you should be able to see changes immediately in the upper portion of the tab view.

In addition to these three options, another option for customization that is offered is the ability to customize the main logo of the login page. You can change the logo image by clicking on the **Browse** button and selecting any image file from your computer. Supported file formats for logo images are .bmp, .jpg, .gif, and .png. Image size should be **410 x 310** pixels. Otherwise, the image will be resized to fit these dimensions. All changes that are made should be saved by clicking on the **Apply** button. If you reopen the Connect login page, you should be able to see all the changes that are applied to this page.

How to customize the meeting room look

In order to change the look of the meeting room, you have to click on the **Customize Meeting** tab.

The **Customize Meeting** tab will help you to create changes for the following items:

- **Menu Highlight Color**
- **Focus Border Color**
- **Background Color**
- **Meeting Main Menu Color**
- **Meeting Main Menu Text Color**
- **Pod Bar Color**
- **Pod Bar Text Color**

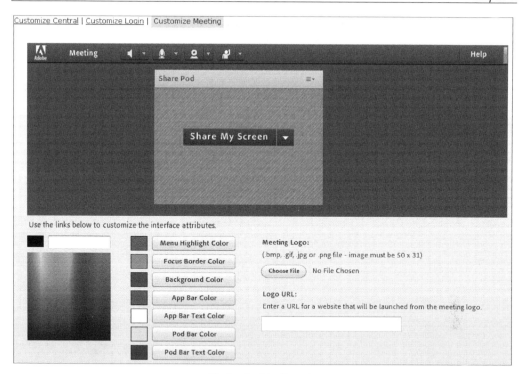

Customize Meeting tab

In the lower-right part of the tab view, you can change the meeting logo. In order to do this, you need to click on the **Choose File** button and select the desired image file from your computer. Supported file formats for logo images are .bmp, .jpg, .gif, and .png. Image size for the meeting logo should be **50 x 31** pixels. An additional option that you can customize is the website URL. You can enter the dedicated URL address for a website, which will be opened when you click on the meeting logo inside the meeting room. As with the previous examples, you will have to click on the **Apply** button to propagate your changes, and you should be able to see the applied changes immediately in the upper section of the tab.

Summary

We have finished the detailed explanation on how to create meeting templates and how to customize certain pages of the Connect application. You should now be able to create various changes in Connect and the meeting room look according to your needs. The next chapter is dedicated to the Content library and how to use it.

5
The Content Library

Adobe Connect has four types of libraries: Meetings, Events, Trainings, and Contents. We will talk about the basics of Adobe Connect's contents. After this chapter, you should have good knowledge about the Content library and how to use different features with this library type.

In this chapter, we will deal with the following topics:

- Working with library files and folders
- Supported file types in the Content library
- Uploading content to the Content library
- Viewing content in the Content library
- Permission settings in the Content library

Working with library files and folders

The Content library contains information about contents that can be easily shared inside the meeting room. Depending on your privileges, which are granted to you by the system administrator, you can add or review different kinds of contents. To navigate to the **Content List** page, click on the **Content** tab on the main menu of the Connect **Home** page.

When you access the page, the content list will be displayed. You will notice that the **Content List** page is similar to the **Meeting List** page, which we described in *Chapter 2, Creating an Adobe Connect Meeting Room*. Since we already described the **Meeting List** page, we will not go through a detailed description of this page. Here, we will show you examples of how to use features available on this page.

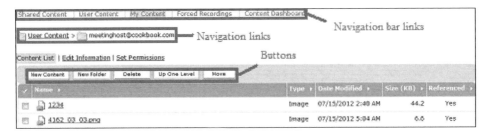

Our first example will show you how to create, delete, or add files and folders, and how to manage them inside the Content library.

In order to add a folder inside the Content library, you should perform the following steps:

1. Navigate to the desired content type by clicking on the content links in the navigation bar. You can select the **Shared Content**, **User Content**, or **My Content** link.

2. Click on the **New Folder** button to open the **New Folder** page.

3. In the **Summary** text area, you can add detailed information about your folder.

4. Enter a name in the **Folder name** text field since this is a mandatory field, and then click on the **Save** button to create a new folder.

To delete a file or a folder, you will have to do the following:

1. Select the desired file or folder by clicking on the checkbox next to it.

2. Click on the **Delete** button so that the **Delete** page will appear.

3. If you want to permanently delete the file or folder, you will have to click on the **Delete** button once again. By clicking on the **Cancel** button, you will cancel the delete process.

To open a folder, click on the folder name; the folders and the files within the selected folder will appear now. The selected folder name will be shown in the navigation links section.

If you want to move the files or folders, you should follow these steps:

1. Click on the checkbox that is on the left-hand side of the desired file or folder.
2. Click on the **Move** button; you will be presented with the **Move** page.
3. On the left-hand side, in the **Items to move** section, the chosen files or folders should be listed.
4. Now, navigate to the folder where you want to move these items. In the **Move to this folder** section, you can review the new location for the files.
5. Click on the **Move** button. When you move the selected folder, all the content within that folder will be moved along to a new location.

On completing these steps, you will get a sound knowledge of how you can organize files and folders inside the Content library according to your needs. Before we go on with the creation of specific content, we will show you the supported file types inside the Content library.

The supported file types in the Content library

In order to add files inside the Content library, they should have one of the following extensions:

- .pdf
- .jpg
- .gif
- .png
- .ppt
- .pptx
- .swf
- .flv
- .html
- .htm
- .mp3
- .mp4
- .f4v

In addition to the listed file formats, you can also upload a ZIP file with specific content. The ZIP files that can be uploaded to the Content library can contain the following formats:

- A ZIP file with `.html` content
- A ZIP file with `.swf` content
- A ZIP file with single `.pdf` content

If you try to upload a file having an unsupported extension, the **Invalid File Format** message will be displayed. Now we can proceed to our next step and teach you how to upload content to the Content library.

Uploading content to the Content library

In order to upload content to the Content library, click on the **New Content** button. When you click on the button, you will be presented with the **Enter Content Information** page. This page is divided into two sections. In the section titled **Select Content File**, click on the **Choose File** button and navigate to a file that you want to upload. Please refer to the following screenshot:

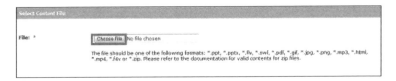

In the lower section titled **Enter content Information**, you have to fill out three fields, namely **Title**, **Custom URL**, and **Summary**. In order to assign a detailed description to the content you wish to upload, you can add some text in the **Summary** field. Similar to the custom URL for the meeting, you can add text in the **Custom URL** text field in order to dedicate a specific URL to your content. If you choose not to create a custom URL, the system will automatically assign a URL to this content. The **Name** field is the only mandatory field, so you will have to populate it. After you complete all the information, click on the **Save** button as shown in the following screenshot:

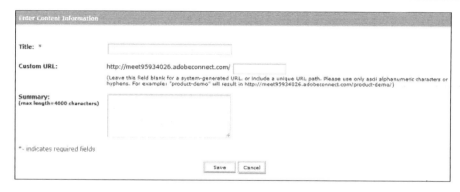

When you click on the **Save** button, you will submit your file to the Content library. Your newly submitted content should now be present in the **Content List** page.

Viewing content in the Content library

In order to view the content information or review previously added content, you need to follow these steps:

1. Navigate to the **Content List** page.

2. Click on the **My content** link in the navigation bar.

3. Go to the **Content Information** page by clicking on the content name in the **Content List** page. You can also access it after clicking on the **Save** button while uploading content. In *Chapter 3, Managing Adobe Connect Meeting Room* we explained how to move a sample file to the Content library; now we will select this file. After we do so, the **Content Information** page will be loaded. In the links section, you can review the items that are linked to your selected content.

4. Click on the URL for viewing the link to view the uploaded image.

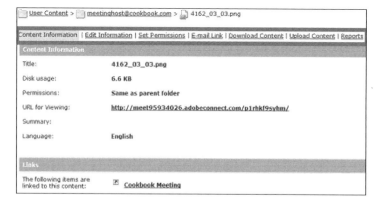

You can note the difference between the navigation bar marked with a red outline in the previous screenshot and the one shown in the screenshot that we presented in *Chapter 3, Managing Adobe Connect Meeting Room*. Following are some functionalities of the navigation bar links:

- **Edit Information**: Here you can edit some attributes of the content that is already uploaded (for example, **Name** and **Summary**).

- **Set Permissions**: This functionality enables you to manage permissions for selected content for a specific user or user group.

- **E-mail Link**: In this tab view you can add e-mail recipients. By selecting the **Send** button, an e-mail message containing the URL link for viewing content will be forwarded to the listed recipients. Note that you may need to log in to your Adobe Connect account in order to view the content. By default, the link sent is not public. You will see in the next chapter how to make sure that your recipients can access the link you sent.

- **Download Content**: When you click on this link, you will be redirected to the **Download Content** page. This page will enable all users that have the permission to access selected content to download this content. Users can simply click on the content name, and the download page will be displayed.

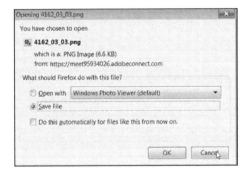

- **Upload Content**: This provides you with the ability to upload new content. The new content that you upload will replace the existing one. In order to do this, the user should follow these instructions:

  i. Click on the **Browse** button and find the location of the new file on your computer.

  ii. Click on the **Save** button.

- **Reports**: In this tab view, the user can find different statistics data in the form of reports regarding the selected content.

Permission settings in the Content library

Administrators and users with appropriate permissions can define which operations are allowed for a specific user or a group whose content exists in the Content library. To manage permission settings, you should go to the **Set Permissions** page. This page can be accessed in two ways. Depending on how you access this page, you can manage permissions for files or folders. In order to change permissions for a folder inside the Content library, navigate to the folder's **Shared Content** option, **My Content** option, and so on of the **Content List** page. Now click on the **Set Permissions** tab. If, on the other hand, you want to change the permission settings for a specific file, this can be achieved by clicking on the **Set Permissions** tab on the **Content Information** page.

We will show you an example on how to manage the rights for the `My content` folder for the administrators group:

1. Navigate to the **Content List** page.

2. Click on the **My Content** link in the navigation bar.

3. Clicking on the **Set Permissions** tab will open the **Set Permissions** page.

4. Select the administrators group in the **Available Users and Groups** table on the left-hand side and click on the **Add** button. Administrators are now added to the **Current Permissions For meetinghost@cookbook.com** table on the right-hand side. Please note that the permission is set to **View** by default.

5. Click on the **Permissions** button, and in the **Permissions** menu choose the **Manage** option.

The following screenshot shows the **Set Permissions** page that illustrates the previous example:

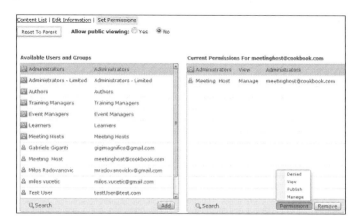

Following are detailed explanations of specific permissions in the **Permissions** menu:

- **Manage**: Users with this permission can view, edit, move, and delete a specific folder or file. These users can also change the permissions for other users, create new folders, and view reports.

- **Publish**: Users and groups with this permission can view, publish, or update presentations as well as view reports. In order to have these capabilities, the users must be members of the **Authors** group. This permission can be granted by an administrator of the Connect application while creating a specific user account.

- **View**: Users and groups granted with this permission can view any content within the folder or any specific file for which they have permissions set.

- **Denied**: Users with this permission cannot view, edit, manage, or publish any file or folder.

In addition to permissions listed previously, you also have the right to allow public viewing of some content. This can be done by selecting the **Yes** radio button next to the label **Allow public viewing**.

Summary

Through this chapter, we introduced you to the Content library. We also went through a couple of examples where we explained contents and the ways they can be edited or organized into folders. We also demonstrated to you how to grant specific privileges to users for desired contents. You should be able to go through the Content library and use the functionalities provided by Adobe Connect.

6
Meeting Room Overview

In the previous chapters we covered functionalities of various pages of Connect. We demonstrated how to create a meeting, edit meeting settings, manage invitees, manage contents, and create a template from any meeting and use it for future meetings. Now, it's time for us to introduce you to the meeting room features and functionalities.

In this chapter, you will learn about:

- Meeting room main menu navigation features
- Keyboard shortcuts and navigation between pods
- Managing attendees through the **Attendees** pod
- Using **Prepare Mode**
- Using **Presenter Only Area**

Meeting room main menu navigation features

At this point you should be familiar with creating, editing, and joining a meeting room; also, we already explained meeting roles to you. Now it is time to go on with further explanations of the meeting room options and functionalities. Depending on your role assigned in a particular meeting, you will have different meeting room options available for use. In case your assigned meeting role is that of the host, the meeting room main menu will look like the following screenshot:

If on the other hand, your assigned meeting role is that of a presenter or participant, the main menu for the meeting room will look like this:

You will notice that the participant and presenter roles have restricted access to host functionalities. Because of this, we will focus on explanation of all host functionalities.

In order to navigate the main menu, the following options are available:

- **Meeting**
- **Layouts**
- **Pods**
- **Audio**

Meeting

Here you will find different options for meeting room management. The following screenshot shows all the options that are available under the **Meeting** menu:

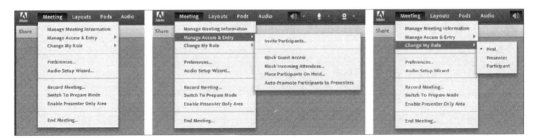

We will describe all the options on this menu:

- **Manage Meeting Information**: Clicking on this option will open the **Meeting Information** page in the Connect application in your default browser. As already described in *Chapter 3, Managing Adobe Connect Meeting Room*, you can edit meeting settings on this page.

- **Manage Access & Entry**: This option will present you with different meeting room management options:

    ◦ **Invite Participants...**: This menu option provides you with features to send invitations to future meeting attendees. Here you will find the meeting URL, and by clicking on the **Compose e-mail** button, your e-mail client will be invoked, and you will be able to compose e-mail for specific participants.

    ◦ **Block Guest Access**: This menu option will disable all the users that are attempting to access a meeting as guests from entering the selected meeting.

    ◦ **Block Incoming Attendees...**: This menu option will prevent users who are trying to join the meeting from entering the meeting room. Users will be prompted with this message, **This meeting is currently in session. The host has blocked entry for incoming attendees.**

    ◦ **Place Participants on Hold**: This menu option will place all incoming attendees on hold. When participants attempt to join a meeting, they will be prompted with this message, **This meeting has been placed on hold. The host will resume the meeting shortly. Thank you.**

    ◦ **Auto-Promote Participants to Presenters**: This menu option will grant presenter rights to the participants present in a meeting room. Additional users who join the selected meeting in the future will automatically be granted with presenter rights as well.

- **Change My Role**: This option reveals a submenu, where you can choose to demote yourself to the presenter or participant role, or on the other hand, to promote yourself to presenter or host.

- **Preferences...**: This option will open the **Preferences** dialog, where you can change different options including **Audio**, **Video**, **Screen Sharing**, **Chat Pod**, **Q & A pod**, and **Attendees Pod**.

- **Audio Setup Wizard**: This will offer options for configuring audio setup.

- **Record Meeting...**: When you click on this option, the host will start to record the specific meeting. Meeting recordings are saved so that they can be reviewed at any time. In *Chapter 12*, *Recording Adobe Connect Meetings*, we will discuss the ability to record Adobe Connect meetings functionality in more detail.

- **Switch To Prepare Mode**: When selected, this option will switch the host to prepare mode; all the changes that he creates while in this mode will not be visible to any meeting attendees.

- **Enable Presenter Only Area**: This option allows the host to add the **Presenter Only Area** features to a currently running meeting. This area will only be visible to users with the host or presenter role.

- **End Meeting...**: By selecting this option, the host can end a meeting that is running currently. When you click on this menu option, the **End Meeting** dialog will appear. This dialog enables you to define a message that will be broadcasted to all participants when the meeting is finished.

Layout

This option gives you the ability to change or customize the look of a meeting room in order to fit your meeting needs. In order to switch to other layouts, a user can choose one of the three options that are offered in the **Layouts** menu.

The options that are offered actually represent three built-in layouts for Adobe Connect, namely, **Sharing**, **Discussion**, and **Collaboration**. If you would like to create a new layout, you should select the option **Create New Layout...**, which is also offered in this menu. In addition to the mentioned options, this menu gives you an option to manage layouts. In case you don't want to save changes to your layout, the **Reset Layouts** option is available for use in this menu. The last option in this menu is the **Close Layout Bar** option. When you click on this option, you will remove the layout bar from the meeting room. We will discuss the **Close Layout Bar** option in depth in *Chapter 11, Customizing and Saving Layouts*. The following screenshot shows the meeting room's **Layouts** and **Pods** menus along with all of the menu options:

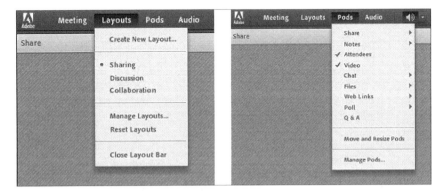

Pods

In this menu item, you will find a list of all the pods that are available, such as:

- **Share**: This pod provides you with functionalities for different sharing options. Here you can choose whether you would like to share your desktop, a whiteboard, or a certain application.

- **Notes**: In this pod, the user can add the meeting agenda or some other information that is considered important for a meeting.

- **Chat**: Using this pod, the user can communicate with other meeting participants. By using this pod, you can send messages to selected users via private conversation or to all of the users via public conversation.

- **Files**: Here you will find options for sharing files inside a meeting room. In this pod, you have an option to upload or download chosen files.

- **Q & A**: This pod contains functionality for questions and answers. In this pod, users can overview opened or answered questions.

- **Poll**: By using this pod in a meeting, you can empower meeting participants to vote in various polls. You can utilize multiple answers, multiple questions, or short-answer polls in this pod.

- **Web Links**: This pod is used for adding web links. Once when you add a web link through this pod, the suggested web page becomes easily accessible to meeting participants in the form of a link provided in the pod.

- **Attendees**: This pod is usually used by the meeting host. By using this pod, the meeting organizer can change participant roles and give additional user rights for selected pods.

- **Video**: This pod enables users with specific rights to start video broadcasting by using their own webcam.

In addition to the list of pods here, you will find the **Manage Pods...** and **Move and Resize Pods** options, which are used to manage pods and to move and resize pods, respectively.

Audio

For this menu option we will cover a scenario in which audio settings are disabled for a meeting. In this case, the menu has only two options: **Microphone Rights for Participants** and **Enable Single Speaker Mode**. By default, microphone rights are only granted to presenters and hosts. By clicking on the **Microphone Rights for Participants** option, the host can change default settings in order to include meeting participants in audio conversations.

When you choose **Enable Single Speaker** mode, an asterisk will appear next to the **Connect My Audio** icon in the main menu. This means that if some user clicks on the **Connect My Audio** option in order to speak, this option will be disabled for all other meeting participants. You will read more about audio menu options when audio is enabled in *Chapter 15, Using Audio and Video.*

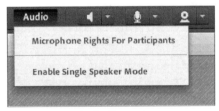

The Audio menu

In addition to the already described main menu meeting room options, you will certainly notice the options shown in the following screenshot:

In order of appearance, these options are:

- **Unmute My Speakers**
- **Connect My Audio**
- **Start My Webcam**
- **Set Status**

You will find more info regarding these options in later chapters.

Keyboard shortcuts and navigating between pods

This topic will teach you how to use keyboard shortcuts for different meeting room pods. By using keyboard shortcuts, one can reduce the use of the mouse to a minimum. All shortcuts presented here are only available for the Windows operating systems. The shortcuts for pods navigation and menus:

- *Ctrl + Space bar*: This shortcut displays the application menu for keyboard navigation
- *Ctrl + F8*: This shortcut displays the **Pod** menu for keyboard navigation

- *Ctrl + F6*: This shortcut moves the focus to the next pod
- *F2*: This shortcut key displays a text field where you can change the title of a pod with a focus on it

Shortcuts for audio and recordings

Refer to the following keyboard shortcuts:

- *Ctrl + M*: This shortcut toggles microphone state between on and off
- *Ctrl + ,*: This shortcut is used to start and stop recording
- *P*: This shortcut is used to toggle the recording state between start and stop when reviewing recordings

Shortcuts for attendee management

Refer to the following keyboard shortcuts:

- *Ctrl + /*: This shortcut promotes user to presenter
- *Ctrl + '*: This shortcut promotes user to host
- *Ctrl +]*: This shortcut demotes user to participant
- *Ctrl + E*: This shortcut toggles the **Raise Hand** status

Shortcuts for dialog boxes

Refer to the following keyboard shortcuts:

- *Esc*: This shortcut key hides, closes, or cancels a dialog box
- *Enter*: This shortcut key executes actions that depend on the dialog box itself

These are the general shortcuts for a meeting room. Beside these general shortcuts, each pod has its own shortcuts.

If you want to use the keyboard to navigate among different pods present in a meeting room, this can be done by clicking on *Ctrl + F6*. By using this command, you change the focus from one pod to another. Please take your time to notice the color of a border around a pod that is in focus. By default, this color is green, as you may see in the following screenshot:

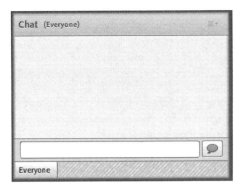

If you'd like to change the border color, you can go back to *Chapter 4, Customizing the Viewing Experience*, where we already described how to perform this.

After joining a meeting, by default, focus is set to the **Chat** pod's message entry text field in cases where the **Chat** pod is present in the meeting.

Managing attendees through the Attendees pod

After explaining the meeting room main menu and overall keyboard shortcuts, we will demonstrate how to manage attendees in the **Attendees** pod. The **Attendees** pod is one of the meeting room pods. It's displayed in all of the default layouts that you can select. The **Attendees** pod is generally placed on the right-hand side of the meeting room and is shown in the following screenshot:

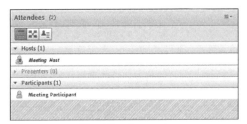

The Attendees pod

At the very top of this pod, you can find a number of attendees that are present in the meeting. In the sample screenshot, this number shows that there are two attendees. In the main part of the **Attendees** pod, every attendee can view who is logged in to a meeting as well as the total count of user roles in a meeting. In the screenshot provided, you can see that there are currently two users that are logged in. One of the users is logged in with the participant role and the other one with a host role. In the example provided, there are no presenters present in this meeting.

Adobe Connect users that are logged in to a meeting with their credentials will appear in the **Attendees** pod. Their name will be displayed; it will be the same name that was used when they were registered by their system administrator for the Adobe Connect application. Users that attend a meeting as guests will have their names displayed in the **Attendees** pod as well. The name that will be displayed for guest attendees is the one they entered when they logged in to the meeting.

Users with the host role can execute specific actions inside this pod. To perform these actions, there are four buttons available to them. These are: **Attendee View**, **Breakout Room View**, **Status View**, and **Pod Options**. We will describe actions that can help hosts to change user roles, remove users from a meeting room, customize attendee names, grant additional rights for specific users on selected pods, and change user status. The following screenshot will help us to explain these actions:

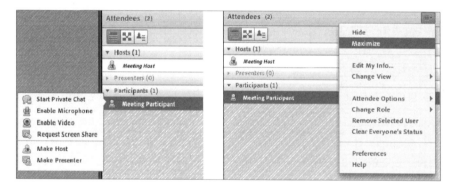

Example 1 – changing user roles

In order to change a user's role, the host should follow these steps:

1. Select the desired meeting attendee in the **Attendees** pod. For the purpose of this example, we will select **Meeting Participant**.

2. Choose a new role for the selected participant by clicking on the **Make Host** or **Make Presenter** menu options.

3. By completing these steps, you have changed the role for the selected meeting participant.

Here is another example of executing the same action:

1. Select a participant and click on the **Pod Options** button. The **Pod** menu should be visible now.

2. In the **Pod** menu, select the **Change Role** menu option.

3. In the submenu, click on **Host, Presenter,** or **Participant.** By completing these steps, you have changed the role for the selected meeting participant.

The easiest way to complete the same action is in just two steps:

1. Select the desired attendee in pod.

2. Drag the selected attendee to a new role.

Example 2 – removing participants

In order to remove a participant from a meeting, the host should follow these steps:

1. Select a participant and click on the **Pod Options** button. The **Pod** menu should appear.

2. Click on the **Remove Selected User** menu option. After completing these steps, the removed user will be prompted with this message: **You have been asked to leave the room.** The removed user will not be present in the **Attendees** pod any more.

Example 3 – editing participant names

In order to edit your own name in the **Attendees** pod, follow these steps:

1. Select your name in the **Attendees** pod and click on the **Pod Options** button.

2. Click on the **Edit My Info...** pod menu option. The **Meeting Participant's Information** dialog should be displayed.

3. In the **Edit Name** text field, enter your new name and click on the **OK** button.

In addition to this action, the meeting host has the ability to change any attendee name. To do so, follow these steps:

1. Select the desired user in the **Attendees** pod and click on the **Pod Options** button.

2. Click on the **Attendee Options** pod menu option.

3. Now, click on the **Edit User Info...** submenu option. The **Meeting Participant's Information** dialog will appear.

4. In **Edit Name** text field, enter a new name for the selected participant, and click on the **OK** button.

Example 4 – granting enhanced participant rights

In this example, we will show you how to grant additional rights for specific pods. By completing this action, the selected participant will be granted with presenter rights for the selected pod without the explicit need to promote the selected participant to presenter. In order to complete this, you can follow these steps:

1. Select the desired user in the **Attendees** pod and click on the **Pod Options** button.

2. Click on the **Attendee Options** pod menu option.

3. Click on the **Enhanced Participant Rights** submenu option. The **Enhanced Participant Rights** dialog box should be presented to you.

4. Click on the checkbox next to the desired pod name, and then click on the **OK** button.

Example 5 – changing meeting attendee status

This example will show you how to change the status in the **Attendees** pod. By default, the status in the **Attendees** pod is blank, but participants can change their statuses.

When a user changes status, an appropriate icon will appear next to the attendee's name. In order to change the status, follow these instructions:

1. Click on the **Set Status** drop-down list in the meeting room main menu.

2. Select the desired status from the status menu as shown in the following screenshot:

Available statuses

The statuses are divided into two groups; **Raise Hand**, **Agree**, **Disagree**, and **Step Away** are in the first group, and **Speak Louder**, **Speak Softer**, **Speed Up**, **Slow Down**, **Laughter**, and **Applause** statuses are in the second group. The statuses from the second group will disappear after 10 seconds. The statuses from the first group will remain in the menu until they are removed manually.

Using Presenter Only Area

In order to enable **Presenter Only Area**, the host needs to follow these steps:

1. Click on the **Meeting** option in the main menu.

2. Click on the **Enable Presenter Only Area** option inside the meeting menu.

After completing this, **Presenter Only Area** is shown on the right-hand side of the meeting room. By default, the **Presenter Notes** pod will be available inside **Presenter Only Area** (as shown in the following screenshot). This area is only visible to hosts and presenters, while it is not visible to participants. It can be used to view confidential content among presenters and hosts and to prepare some content before sharing it with other meeting participants. Additionally, the host can add any pod to **Presenter Only Area**, and this action will not be seen by the participants. In order to disable **Presenter Only Area**, please follow these steps:

1. Click on the **Meeting** option in the main menu.

2. Click on the **Disable Presenter Only Area** option inside the meeting menu.

When you complete these steps, the Presenter Only area will be removed from the meeting room.

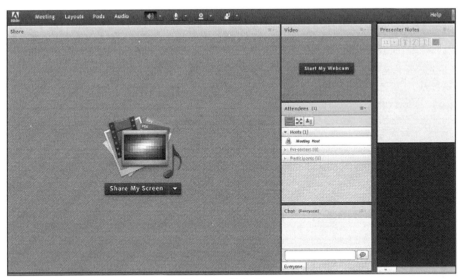

Presenter Only Area

Using Prepare Mode

Prepare Mode helps meeting hosts to adjust the visual appearance of non-active layouts without affecting the active layout currently seen by attendees. In order to open the prepare mode, select **Meeting** from the main menu and click on the **Switch to Prepare Mode** option. A notification message will show up, informing you that you are in **Prepare Mode** now. Another indicator that you are in **Prepare Mode** is a yellow border around the meeting area. From the **Layouts** menu or the **Layout** bar, select the layout that you would like to adjust. Afterwards, you can move, hide, or show pods as needed.

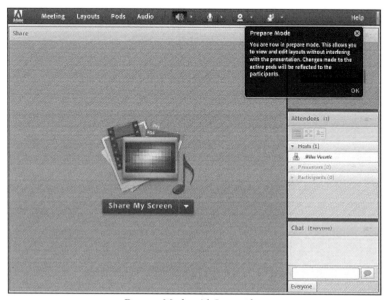

Prepare Mode with Layout bar

When you are finished adjusting the layout, choose the **Meeting** option from the main menu and click on the **End Prepare Mode** option in order to close it.

Now that you have selected the layout that you have adjusted in **Prepare Mode**, all changes will be presented to meeting attendees.

Summary

This chapter has taught you how to use different options provided by meeting room menus. We also covered **Presenter Only Area**, **Prepare Mode**, and the **Attendees** pod, where we saw a couple of examples of how these features might be used. The next chapter will give you more info about how you may share presentations within Connect meeting rooms.

7
Sharing Presentations

In this chapter you will get familiar with the **Share** pod and learn how to use some of its basic functionalities. The central topic of this chapter will be sharing of presentations, and after reading this chapter, you will be able to share, customize, and navigate through presentations within the **Share** pod.

In this chapter, we will cover the following areas:

- The **Share** pod
- Presentation toolbar options
- Navigation through presentations

The Share pod

Now that you are familiar with creating meetings, entering meetings, and using the meeting room main menu navigation, we will start with meeting room pods and their functions.

We have discussed meeting room templates in some of the previous chapters, while we have also written about three default meeting layouts: **Sharing**, **Discussion**, and **Collaboration** layouts. By default, a newly created meeting will be set up with the **Sharing** layout, and the central pod for this layout will be the **Share** pod.

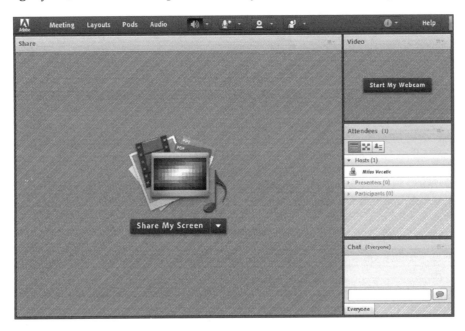

The **Share** pod provides you with several different sharing options, such as:

- Sharing for various document formats (supported formats are listed in *Chapter 5, The Content Library*)
- Sharing your computer screen
- Sharing the whiteboard

Our focus in this chapter will be on the document sharing option in order to describe presentation sharing by using the **Share** pod.

There are two ways in which you can start presentation sharing. At the center of the **Share** pod, you will find a quick launch menu with several options for sharing. One of them is the **Document** sharing option. In addition to this option, you will find the **Pod** menu with the same option located in the top-right corner of the **Share** pod.

Please see the following screenshot:

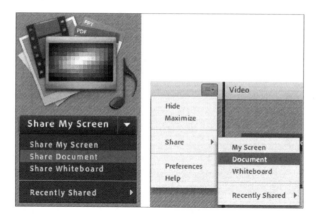

Once you select one of these options, you will be presented with the **Select Document to Share** pop-up window as shown the following screenshot:

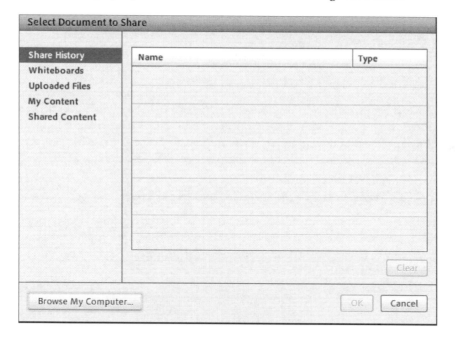

A menu will be displayed on the left-hand side of the pop-up window, and here you will find several options listed:

- **Browse My Computer…**: You will find this button in the bottom-left corner. By clicking on this button, you can upload documents directly from your computer instead of using contents uploaded in the Content library as described in *Chapter 5, The Content Library*.

  Please note that loading content directly from the computer takes a little longer that loading it from the Content library.

- **Share History**: This option will display a list of previously shared documents by using the **Share** pod. This list will show details such as the document name and the type of document that was shared.

- **Whiteboards**: This section contains a list of available **Whiteboards** pods that a user can share by using the **Share** pod.

- **Uploaded Files**: This option will list all documents that were previously uploaded by using the **Browse My Computer…** button.

- **My Content**: This section provides a list of your documents that were uploaded to the Content library.

- **Shared Content**: This section will provide a list of shared documents uploaded to the Content library by other users.

For demonstration purposes, in this chapter, we will share a presentation directly from the computer. You can also share a presentation by using a document that is already uploaded to the Content library (as described in *Chapter 5, The Content Library*).

Presentation toolbar options

After selecting the PowerPoint file you would like to share, you will see the **Converting…** message with a progress bar shown in the center of the **Share** pod. This progress bar is an indicator of the remaining time that is needed to load the presentation.

After successful conversion, you will be presented with the presentation file you have selected. In order to illustrate this option, we have created a sample PowerPoint file to be used for this chapter.

Once the presentation is loaded, several different buttons will appear in the **Share** pod. All of these options can also be found in the context menu of the **Share** pod, located in the upper-right corner of the **Share** pod.

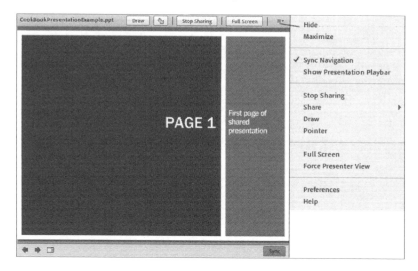

The following table will describe functionalities that are invoked by the buttons in the list:

Button	Description
Draw	The **Draw** button enables whiteboard functionalities for shared presentations.
(pointer icon)	The **Pointer** button places a pointer icon on the desired area within the presentation.
Stop Sharing	The **Stop Sharing** button stops presentation sharing.
Full Screen	The **Full Screen** button opens presentation sharing in full screen mode.

Button	Description
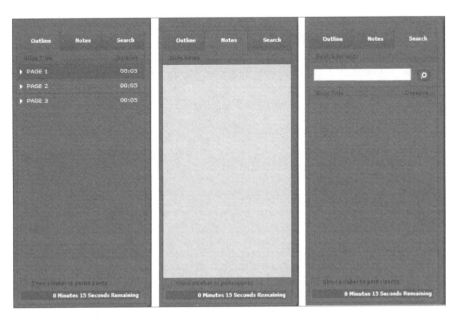	The navigation arrows allow you to navigate through different presentation slides. You can also use the keyboard arrow keys for this purpose.
	The **Show Side Bar** button opens a side bar on the right-hand side of the presentation.
	The **Sync** button toggles sharing synchronization with other attendees on and off.

Navigation through presentations

You can navigate through any presentation by using the navigation arrows that are placed in the bottom-left corner of the **Share** pod. By clicking on the **Show Side Bar** button, you can open a side bar on the right-hand side of the shared presentation. This side bar will show some detailed information about the presentation. There are three different tabs in the side bar:

- The **Outline** tab will show you a list of all slides in your presentation, with information about their names and durations. On this tab, you can navigate through slides by selecting an individual slide from the list. This sidebar is only visible to hosts and presenters. They can enable this sidebar for all attendees by selecting a checkbox next to the **Show Side Bar to participants** checkbox at the bottom of the sidebar.

- In the **Notes** tab, you will find notes for the slide selected on the first side bar (if there are any). Notes from the PowerPoint presentation will automatically be imported here.

- The **Search** tab will help you to search through the text of a shared presentation. You can find content by entering sample text that you would like to locate in a presentation.

Please note that, once shared, a presentation remains visible in the **Share** pod until **Stop Sharing** is hit. The presentation will remain visible even if the meeting room is closed.

Summary

In this chapter we demonstrated how to use some of the basic functionalities of the **Share** pod. Also, we explained how to upload a presentation document and how to navigate through different slides of a presentation. You are now familiar with using the **Share** pod for successful presentation sharing. In the next chapter, we will familiarize you with the functionalities of the whiteboard feature.

8

Using a Whiteboard Feature in the Meeting Room

In this chapter, we will cover most of the functionalities for successful usage of the whiteboard pod. After completing this chapter, you will be ready to use a whiteboard and all of its drawing tools.

Over the course of this chapter you will learn how to:

- Create and display a whiteboard
- Use whiteboard drawing tools

Create and display a whiteboard

Whiteboard is a part of the share pod. It provides various drawing features within meeting room. It allows hosts or presenters to create text, lines, circles, squares, and other freehand drawings in real time during a meeting.

There are two different ways to use the whiteboard:

- Using the standalone whiteboard, which creates content on the white background
- Using a whiteboard as an overlay of a sharing document in the share pod, which enables users to add drawings and annotations over documents

Standalone whiteboard

You can create a standalone whiteboard in two different ways, as follows:

- In the share pod, click on **Pod Options | Share | Whiteboard**
- In the share pod, click on **Share My Screen | Share Whiteboard**

These options are shown in the following screenshots:

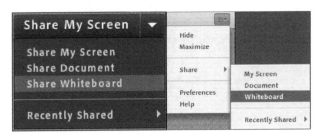

After selecting one of these options you will be presented with the whiteboard pod. You will notice that the sharing has already started and the title of your share pod has been changed to whiteboard. As you can see in the following screenshot, toolbar with several options appears in the upper-left corner of the whiteboard. We will go through all of these tools in the next topic. Also, some of the buttons that we previously described in *Chapter 7, Sharing Presentations*, appear in the upper-right corner:

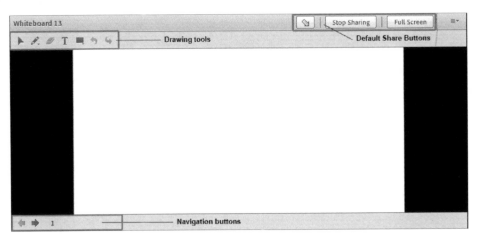

A standalone whiteboard contains multiple pages, for example, a regular flip board. You can navigate through these pages by using navigation arrows in the lower-left corner. You can also jump to a particular page by entering the page number in the text field. This option is available only in the standalone whiteboard.

In order to display an already existing whiteboard, from the main menu select **Pods | Share** and select the name of the whiteboard.

Adding an overlay whiteboard in a share pod

In order to add a whiteboard as an overlay of a shared document, you need to click on the **Draw** button in the share pod.

The share pod provides you with an option to pause screen sharing and annotate by using the whiteboard. We will describe this feature in detail in the next chapter.

After you've clicked on the **Draw** button, a whiteboard turns on with all of its tools enabled in the upper-left corner of the pod, as shown in the following screenshot:

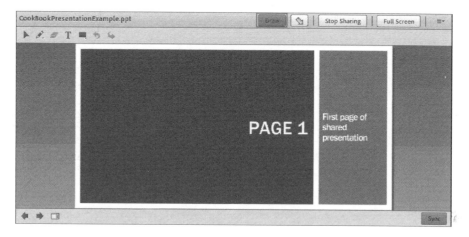

In case you've added some drawings, hitting the **Draw** button again will hide the drawings added to a slide. It does not erase them. Thus it is possible to mask a whole graph and display it later on the slide. And since Adobe Connect remembers what you draw on a presentation (as long as you do not stop sharing), you'll keep your drawing forever!

Whiteboard drawing tools

Whiteboard drawing tools are used to create text and drawings on the whiteboard. Tools that are available are **Shapes**, **Selection**, **Pencil**, **Text**, and the **Delete Selected**, **Undo**, and **Redo** buttons.

The Shapes tool

The **Shapes** tool is used to create different shapes on the whiteboard. By clicking on the shapes tool button, the tool will display a list of different shapes. Once you select one of the shapes that are available, the customizing appearance tool will be enabled on the right-hand side of the toolbar. You can select border and background color as well as option for border thickness. You can click on the control points on the selected rectangle and drag them to expand the shape. In order to create an even width and height for selected shapes you will need to hold down the *Shift* key while dragging the mouse.

The Selection tool

The **Selection** tool is used to select a desired shape or area on the whiteboard. In order to use it, click on a shape to select it. The selection rectangle has eight control points for resizing the selected shape and one point that is used for shape rotation. Shift and drag a corner control point to maintain the aspect ratio when you resize the shape. In order to add text to the shape you need to double-click on it, and a textbox will appear. Select and drag a shape to move it around.

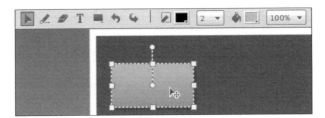

The Pencil tool

The **Pencil** tool is used to create a freeform line. You can customize stroke color and stroke weight by using the color picker and the **Stroke weight** pop-up menu. The menu will appear when you select the **Pencil** tool. Additionally, you can select a **Highlighter** option by holding the pencil tool button. A drop-down menu will appear and you will be able to select the **Pencil** or **Highlighter** tool (please see the following screenshot).

The Text tool

The **Text** tool allows you to create a floating multiline text field. You can customize text fill color, font face, and font size by using the color picker, the **Font** pop-up menu, and the **Font size** pop-up menu, respectively.

The Delete Selected button

The **Delete Selected** button is enabled when you select a drawn object by using the **Selection** tool. By clicking on it, you will delete the selected object.

The Undo button

The **Undo** button deletes current changes on the whiteboard. You can undo the actions such as shape drawing, moving a shape, resizing a shape, clearing the whiteboard, and changing a shape's property. There is no limit to the number of times that you can perform the undo operation in the pod. By using this button it is also possible to delete an object individually, whenever it has been created.

The Redo button

The **Redo** button reverses the undo action on the whiteboard.

Beside these whiteboard drawing tools, you will find one very useful option inside the pod option menu. This option is **Print**. Since a drawing created within Connect can't be exported, use this option to print the drawing.

Summary

In this chapter you have learned how to use the whiteboard pod as a standalone pod as well as an overlay of a document that is already shared within the share pod. Now you can create and customize different shapes and text by using the whiteboard features. In the next chapter we will cover screen sharing together with all the functionalities of this feature.

9
Using Screen Sharing

During this chapter, we will cover most of the screen sharing functionalities of share pods. After completing this chapter, you will be ready to use various screen sharing options available in share pods.

In this chapter, we will cover the following topics:

- Starting screen sharing
- Desktop sharing
- Applications and window sharing
- Systray sharing options
- Share pod preferences

Starting screen sharing

In the previous chapter we have described the sharing of documents and whiteboards using share pod. Besides these sharing types, share pod allows you to share your screen. As before, you can start screen sharing by selecting the **Share My Screen** option from the quick launch menu or from the context menu of a share pod. After selecting one of these options you will be presented with the **Start Screen Sharing** dialog box.

Please note that screen sharing is only available while running a meeting using the connect add-in. In case you are running a meeting room using only the browser application, clicking on **Start Screen Sharing** will prompt you to install the connect add-in and will automatically reload the meeting room using the connect add-in.

In the **Start Screen Sharing** dialog box, you will find several options, as shown in the following screenshot:

As you can see, there are three different options for screen sharing, as follows:

- **Desktop**
- **Applications**
- **Windows**

For each one of these you have additional options, which we will see in the next section.

Desktop sharing

Selecting the **Desktop** sharing option allows you to share the contents of your desktop. If you have more than one monitor connected to your computer, a desktop icon appears for each monitor. Choose the desktop that you want to share. Note that, if needed, you can change the monitor shared once sharing is activated. You will see how to do that in the following section.

When you start your screen, the sharing message, **Your screen is being shared** appears and the name of the share pod will change in a way that the name of the attendee who is sharing screen will be appended to the name of the share pod. In order to make sure your audience see what you are sharing correctly, you can switch your pod to full screen and force presenter view.

Please note that screen sharing means that your whole screen will be shrunk in the relatively smaller share pod. Thus, if you have a fairly large screen (larger than average), reducing its resolution will help your audience see your content properly.

Changing control of a shared screen

While screen sharing, you can pass control of the shared desktop, window, or application to another host or presenter.

The instance you start sharing your screen, a **Request Control** button will appear in the share pod of the other hosts and presenters in the meeting. Only users with presenter and host rights or users with specific rights granted for the share pod will have this button in the upper-right corner of share pod:

If you click on this button, a notification message will appear both for user who is sharing and for user who is requesting control, as shown in the following screenshots:

When hosts and presenters request control of the screen, the user who is sharing must grant the request. Control cannot be taken without permission.

If for request for control is granted, the **Release Control** button will appear instead of the **Request Control** button and a notification message will appear, as shown in the following screenshots:

Clicking on the **Release Control** button on the share pod will return control of the shared screen to the original host or presenter. Also a notification message will pop up, as follows:

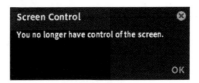

Applications and window sharing

The share pod provides you with an option to share just certain applications you choose. If you select the **Applications** option from the **Start Screen Sharing** dialog box, the list of applications running on your computer will be presented to you. Selecting one or more of them will share an application and all its related windows that are open and running on your computer.

Selecting the **Windows** sharing option allows you to share one or more windows that are open and running on your computer.

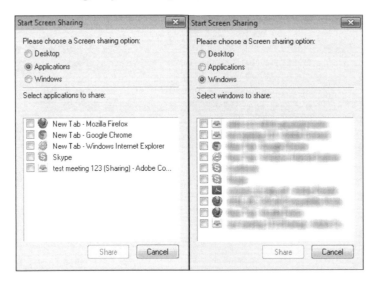

The same changing control options apply to application and windows sharing.

When screen sharing starts, the systray icon appears in the taskbar of your computer, providing you several different options. In the next section we will explain this in detail.

Systray sharing options

On screen sharing start in the taskbar of your computer will appear systray icon of connect application, as shown in the following screenshot:

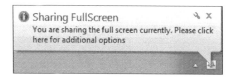

If you click on this icon, a menu with different options will appear. We will now go through each one of these. See the following screenshot:

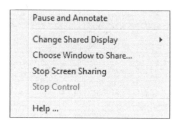

The following are the available options:

- **Pause and Annotate**: If you remember we spoke about this option in *Chapter 8, Using a Whiteboard Feature in the Meeting Room,* where we have described using whiteboards. Clicking on this option will open a whiteboard as an overlay of a shared screen in a share pod. You will be able to use all whiteboard tools in order to focus other attendees' attention to the part of the shared screen that you want. You will also notice that in the options of the systray icon now you have the **Resume Sharing** option instead of **Pause and Annotate**. Clicking on this will resume your screen sharing. Note that the annotations will be lost, unless you print them out before resuming.

- **Change Shared Display**: If you are in the desktop sharing mode, you will find the **Change Shared Display** option, which allows you to change a shared monitor if you have one.

- **Choose Window to Share...**: Also, you can easily switch to the window sharing mode by clicking on the **Choose Window to Share...** option in the menu of the systray icon.

- **Stop Screen Sharing** and **Stop Control**: These shared screen options are also available in this menu.

Share pod preferences

In order to optimize screen sharing quality, you will need to open the share pod's **Preferences** dialog box. In the share pod context menu click on the **Preferences** option.

You will be presented with the **Preferences** dialog box. In this dialog box you can set the **Quality** and **Frame Rate** for your screen sharing.

For example, if there are large delays before attendees see changes to a shared screen, reduce the **Quality** setting. Or, if smooth motion is essential for a video you are sharing, increase **Frame Rate**. See the following screenshot:

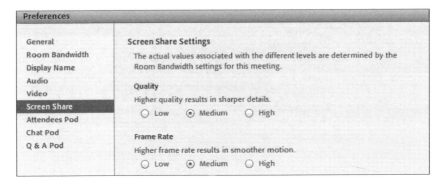

Summary

During this chapter you have learned how to use screen sharing options. You can now successfully share your desktop, applications, and windows using a share pod. Also you learned how to use whiteboard features while sharing your screen. We have also gone through some basics about setting sharing quality using the **Preferences** dialog box. Now you are ready to use a share pod with all of its functionalities, sharing documents, whiteboards, and screens.

10
Customizing Pod Display

In this chapter, we will go through:

- The **Pods** menu description
- The pod's **Preferences** dialog
- Managing pods

In this chapter, you will learn how to adjust your layouts by displaying different pods in it. We will talk about context menu of pods and about the pods **Preferences** dialog.

The Pods menu description

During previous chapters, while we were talking about share pods, we spoke about context menu. Every pod in a meeting room (chat, note, web links, poll pod, and so on) has its own context menu with different menu options depending on pod type. For each pod, the context menu has some specific options, and some common options that are placed in the context menu of every pod. In order to open a context menu, you need to click on a button placed in the upper-right corner of each pod. We can see three different sections in each context menu. See the following screenshot:

The options in the first and third sections are common for context menus of each pod. In the first section there are options for hiding, maximizing, and restoring pods. In the third section you will find help options, which are linked to the online help, and you will also find a preferences option that displays a **Preferences** dialog box where you can set some additional options for each pod.

In the middle section you will find options specific for each pod. We will explain in detail these options when we come to chapters for each pod.

The pod's Preferences dialog

By clicking on the **Preferences** option in the context menu of each pod, the user will be presented with the **Preference** pop-up dialog box. You can also open this dialog box by clicking on the **Meeting** option in the main menu of the meeting room and then the **Preferences** option. See the next screenshot:

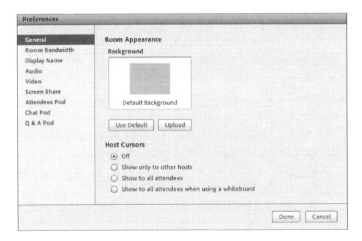

Within the left-hand side of this dialog box, you will find nine tabs for adjusting additional options of meeting room and meeting room pods. Note that in this dialog box there are options such as **Video**, **Screen Share**, **Attendees Pod**, **Chat Pod**, and **Q & A Pod**. Also, only in context menu of these pods, you will find preferences options mentioned before.

Besides pod options there are some general settings for **Room Appearance**, **Room Bandwidth**, and **Audio Settings**.

Managing pods

Each of the default layouts has its own pods placed in certain locations within meeting room. Hosts can show, hide, add, delete, rearrange, and organize pods. More than one instance of a pod (except **Attendees Pod** and **Video**) can be displayed in a meeting at the same time. From the **Pods** menu you can add new pods, hide and show already existing pods. See the next screenshot:

To show a pod, select it from the **Pods** menu; note here that a pod will appear in **Presenter Only Area** when it is enabled. For pods that can have multiple instances, select the instance name from the submenu. A check mark appears next to the names of pods that are currently visible in the meeting. To hide a pod, deselect it in the **Pods** menu, or click on the menu icon in the upper-right corner of the pod and choose **Hide**.

You can also display a pod at maximum size. When you maximize a pod, it expands to fill the whole meeting room (either within the browser window or when the add-in is used). You can do this by clicking on the **Maximize** option in the context menu of a pod. In order to restore pod size, just click on the **Restore** option in the context menu of a pod.

In the **Pods** menu of the **Main Menu** bar, you will found the **Add New** option for each pod type. Clicking on it will automatically add a new pod instance to the existing meeting room. Also, in the previous screenshot, you can see that each instance of a selected pod type is listed in the **Pods** menu.

In this menu you will also find the **Move and Resize Pods** option. By enabling it, you will be able to move and resize your pods in the meeting room area. To move a pod, drag it by its title bar. To resize a pod, drag any corner or side. Remember that only hosts can manage pods. Neither participants nor presenters can do so.

Organize pods

You can see the full list of existing pods in the **Manage Pods** dialog. In the menu bar, follow these steps:

1. Select **Pods**.

2. Click on **Manage Pods**.

   You will be presented with the **Dialog** pop up. See the following screenshot:

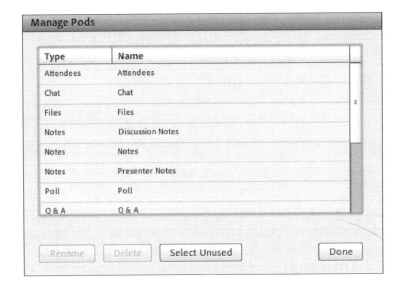

Here you can see the list of all pods created in the meeting room. The first column contains information about pod type and the second contains the name of the pod instance created in the meeting. Using this dialog box you can rename or remove selected pods from the list. This dialog box also allows you to easily detect which of the pods from the meeting room are currently unused by clicking on the **Select Unused** button. After that, all unused pods will be selected. See the following screenshot:

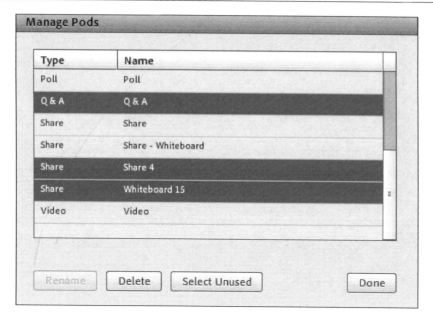

3. Now you can delete all of them by clicking on the **Delete** button. Hitting **Done** will close the window anytime.

Summary

In this chapter we have covered basics for managing meeting room pods. Now you can easily adjust meeting room layouts according to your needs. You can add, remove, resize, move, hide, and show pods within the meeting room. In next chapter we will cover some more features for customizing and managing layouts.

11
Customizing and Saving Layouts

In this chapter you will learn how to create and manage layouts of meeting room. This will help you adjust the meeting room's appearance and save changes for future meeting sessions. Moreover, the use of layouts will automatically enhance the table of content of recordings.

In this chapter, we will go through the following topics:

- Creating layouts
- Managing layouts
- Changing and managing layouts during a meeting

Creating layouts

In order to create a new layout you will use the layout menu presented in the main menu of a meeting room or the layout bar placed on the right-hand side of a meeting room. Both, the layout menu and layout bar, are visible only to attendees with host rights.

To create a blank layout on which you can manually add pods, go to the main menu and click on the **Layouts** tab. In the layout menu select the **Create new layout...** option. Another way is to click on the **+** button in the lower-right corner of the layout bar, as shown in the following screenshots:

After selecting one of these options you will be presented with the **Create a New Layout** dialog box. In this dialog box you are provided with two different options for creating a new layout. You can create a blank layout or you can duplicate an existing layout. Below these options is the text input field for entering the new layout name, as shown in the following screenshot:

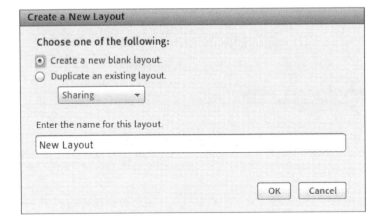

Selecting the first option for creating a layout will automatically set the new created layout to active, and the meeting room area will be empty, without any pods inside it. Selecting the second option will create a new layout based on the layout selected in the combo box. Clicking on the **OK** button will automatically set this layout to active and all pods from the layout you have copied will be present at the same location and with the same size in the meeting room area.

In the layout menu as well as on the layout bar you can see which layout is currently active. In the following screenshots you can see that the newly created layout, which we called **Test Layout**, is now present and active:

Managing layouts

The default layouts are the **Sharing**, **Discussion**, and **Collaboration** layouts. You can easily delete, rename, or change the order of layouts.

To rename a layout go to the layouts menu and click on the **Manage Layouts** option. In the **Manage Layouts** dialog box you will be presented with the options to select the layout you want to rename. Click on the **Rename** button to change the name.

You can also rename the layout by double-clicking on the layout in the layout bar. In this dialog box you can also arrange the layout order. Just select the layout and click on the up or down buttons to reorder layouts. Please note that you can reorder layouts by simply dragging a layout in the layout bar to a desired position. See the following screenshots:

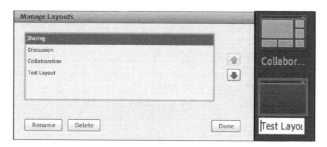

Similarly, you can delete layouts using the **Delete** button. Note that if you delete the layout that is currently in use, the default sharing layout will be applied to the meeting.

Changing and managing layouts during a meeting

The layout menu and the layout bar are visible only to hosts. The default layouts are **Sharing**, **Discussion**, and **Collaboration**. Any custom layouts are also listed. The layout bar also displays thumbnails for the layouts. When a host chooses a different layout, the new layout appears on every attendee's screen. You can switch to another layout by clicking on the layout name in the layout menu or selecting layout from the layout bar.

 Please note that if all the layouts do not fit in the layout bar to scroll through the layouts, hover the pointer over the first or the last layout previews. You can also use the panning options or the mouse wheel to scroll through.

You can also adjust a layout during a meeting without affecting the active layout currently seen by other attendees. To do this, select **Meeting** from the main menu and click on the **Switch to Prepare Mode** option. From the layout menu or the layout bar, select the layout that you would like to adjust. Afterwards, you can move, hide, or show pods as needed. When you are finished with adjusting the layout, choose the **Meeting** option from the main menu and click on the **End Prepare Mode** option in order to close it. Then, you will be back to the layout you quit while activating **Prepare Mode**. **Prepare Mode** is described in detail in *Chapter 6, Meeting Room Overview*.

Reset layouts to revert to the default layouts. Any modifications to the **Sharing**, **Discussion**, and **Collaboration** layouts are reverted, and custom layouts are deleted. To do this in the layout menu click on the **Reset Layout** option. The confirmation dialog box will appear. Clicking on **Reset** will reset default layouts to a default state.

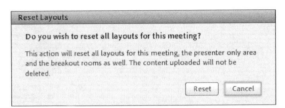

Please note that you cannot reset layouts if a meeting is being recorded.

Specifying layout bar options

Layout bar options let you specify the docking position and auto hide settings. By clicking on the button in the upper-left corner of layout bar, you can see available options for the layout bar, as shown in the following screenshot:

The following are the available options:

- **Dock to the left**: Enables docking the layout bar to the left-hand side of the meeting room window.

- **Dock to the right**: Enables docking the layout bar to the right-hand side edge of the meeting room window.

- **Auto Hide**: Enables auto hiding the layout bar. Click on this option to pull out the layout bar.

Summary

In this chapter you learned how to create and manage meeting room layouts. Now after reading both this and the previous chapters you can easily adjust your meeting room appearance and save those settings for future meeting sessions. We have also covered most of the functionalities of the layout bar and learned how to quickly adjust a meeting room layout using these features.

12
Recording Adobe Connect Meetings

In this chapter we will demonstrate how you can record meeting, manage meeting recordings, and review and edit particular meeting recording. By the end of this chapter you will have adequate knowledge about applicable recording features for meetings included in the Connect application. In this chapter, we will explain to you how to:

- Record a meeting
- Manage recorded meetings
- Play back recorded meeting
- Edit a recorded meeting
- Create an offline recording

Recording a meeting

In order to start recording a meeting, a user must have a host role in a meeting. It is important to note that all of the actions, that are performed inside a meeting room will be recorded. The only exceptions to this rule are Presenter Only Area, which has been already described in *Chapter 6, Meeting Room Overview,* and breakout rooms, which will be described in detail in later chapters of this book. When a meeting is played back, recording will contain the exact events that meeting attendees were able to see or hear while recording a meeting. Additionally, by reviewing a recording you should be able to review meeting attendees and their roles. In order to start recording your meeting you should perform the following steps:

1. Click on the **Meeting** option in the meeting room main menu.
2. Click on the **Record Meeting...** option.

3. The **Record Meeting** dialog box will pop up.

4. In the **Name** textbox you can enter your recording name and in the **Summary** textbox you have the option to add a more detailed description of a specific recording.

5. Click on the **OK** button.

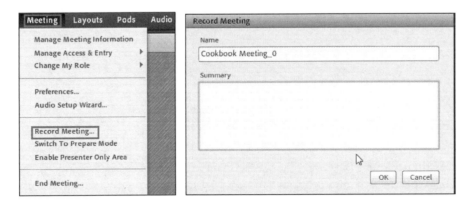

After a meeting recording is started, you should be able to see the red dot in the meeting room main menu on the far right, as shown in the following screenshot:

This red dot is an indicator that your meeting is being recorded. It is also important to mention here that the host can start or stop meeting recording at any given time during the meeting. Every meeting recording is associated with a unique URL address, which is assigned automatically and will be saved in the recording list of meetings in the **Recordings** tab on the **Meeting Information** page.

Managing meeting recordings

In order to manage recordings associated with a meeting, you will need to navigate to the **Meeting Information** page for a specific meeting as we already described in *Chapter 3, Managing Adobe Connect Meeting Room*. When you navigate to the **Meeting Information** page, click on the **Recordings** tab marked with a red outline, as shown in the following screenshot. When you complete this action, the **Recordings** page will load.

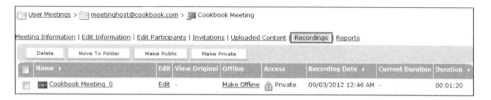

This page will provide you with functionalities that will enable you to manage or edit specific recordings for the meeting. We will teach you how to delete existing recording, edit recording information, move a particular recording to a different folder, and create recordings that are available for public viewing.

Deleting recordings

To delete an already existing recording, users should perform the following steps:

1. Click on the checkbox to the left-hand side of the desired recording name; see the preceding screenshot.

2. Click on the **Delete** button.

3. You will be redirected to the confirmation page; then click on the **Delete** button again.

4. By completing this you will permanently delete the selected meeting recording.

Moving recordings

This operation is very similar to any other move operation that is already described in this book. In order to move the recording, you will need to perform the following steps:

1. Click on the checkbox to the left-hand side of any recording that you want to move to another location.

2. Click on the **Move To Folder** button.

3. You are now on the **Move To Folder** page.

4. In the **Move To This Folder** section in the right-hand part of this page, navigate to the location to which you would like to transfer the chosen recording or multiple recordings.

5. Click on the **Move** button.

6. You will be prompted with the message – **The following items were moved successfully**.

Enabling recordings for public viewing

To enable public viewing of a recording you will need to perform the following steps:

1. Click on the checkbox on the left-hand side of the chosen recording name.

2. Click on the **Make Public** button.

3. After completing these steps, you should see that the value will be changed in the **Access** column from **Private** to **Public**.

The following screenshot outlines the preceding steps:

When the access to a recording is set to **Public**, anyone who has the recording URL address will be able to review it without the need to log in to the Connect application. If you switch the access to the meeting recording back to **Private** by clicking on the **Make Private** button, users will need to log in to Connect before they can view the meeting recording.

Editing recording information

In order to edit recording information you should execute the following steps:

1. Click on the preferred recording name in the recordings list.

2. The **Recording Information** page will be displayed to you. On this page you can review recording data including recording duration, recording name, summary, and the recording URL.

3. In the recording information bar click on the **Edit** link.

4. Change the recording name, summary, or language and click on the **Save** button.

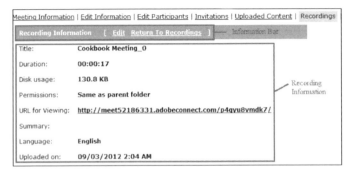

Playing back a recorded meeting

By now, we've demonstrated that once the meeting is recorded, it can be reviewed multiple times until the recording is deleted, as described previously. In order to play back an already existing recording navigate to the **Recording Information** page as shown in the preceding screenshot and click on the **URL For Viewing** link. By doing this you will start the recorded meeting. In addition to the actions and events recorded in a meeting, users should be able to see a recording navigation bar in the bottom part of the window of played back recording. The recording navigation bar should look similar to the one shown in the following screenshot:

The recording navigation bar contains the following functional buttons:

- **Start/Pause button**: This button toggles between recording play/pause states.
- **Progress marker**: The users can use this functionality to jump to a desired position. This can be done by dragging the pointer marker on the progress bar.
- **Elapsed/Total time marker**: This displays total recording length and current progress marker position.
- **Volume control button**: The users can adjust volume levels by dragging the button in order to increase/decrease volume.

Furthermore, there is an additional functionality that enables users to navigate throughout recordings. This functionality allows users to navigate to a specific event in recordings. Events that are captured in recording include chat messages, layout changes, slide changes, and attendee's changes. In order to use this navigation option, you will need to click on the little triangle on the left-hand side of the window where recording is played back. After clicking on the triangle, you should see the **Events Index** panel, as shown in the following screenshot:

In this panel you can navigate to a specific meeting event that was recorded (for example, a layout change). In addition, this panel contains the **Filter Events** pop-up menu. By using filters, users can list all recorded events, a specific event, or multiple selections of the captured events. The **Events Index** panel contains the **Search** functionality, so you can perform various event searches inside the recording. By describing this panel, we have finished our review of the functionalities associated with recording playback. The next step for us is to demonstrate to you how to edit meeting recording.

Editing recorded meeting

In this section we will focus on functionalities and ways to edit already existing meeting recording. This functionality is very useful in cases where there is plenty of silence inside the meeting that has been recorded. In order to eliminate parts with usual silence during the recording, users can modify parts of the recording where silence is present. We will explain two ways to start recording in the edit mode, as follows:

- The first method to start recording in the edit mode is by clicking on the **Edit** button in recordings table associated with a specific meeting. The **Edit** button is marked with a red outline in the following screenshot:

- The second method to execute the same operation is to click on the **Edit** button on the **Recording Information** page. You can see a sample of this page and how to navigate to it in the *Managing meeting recordings* section.

After you start recording in the edit mode, instead of seeing the recording navigation bar described previously, now you will see the bar with slight changes:

This bar contains an additional four buttons: **Cut**, **Undo**, **Save**, and **REVERT TO ORIGINAL**, and selection markers. In order to edit a meeting recording by using this bar, users can perform the following steps:

1. Use selection markers to select a certain position in the recording that you want to remove from it.

2. Click on the **Cut** button.

3. After doing this, in order to permanently save changes, users will need to click on the **Save** button.

4. As a form of verification that changes were made successfully, users should be able to see changes in the total recording length after the playback restart.

After the changes to the recording are made, the **REVERT TO ORIGINAL** button will be enabled. If for some reason you realize that changes made to a recording were incorrect, you can click on the **REVERT TO ORIGINAL** button. By using this button, users can remove the applied changes to the recording and restore the original meeting recording no matter how many changes were made. Compared to the **REVERT TO ORIGINAL** button, the **Undo** button will only revert the last change applied to the meeting recording.

Users can edit meeting recording as many times as needed. In the meantime, the URL for the recording will always remain the same. Once the changes to a recording are made and saved successfully, the **View Original** column in the recording table field will be populated. You can notice the difference by comparing the screenshot on the previous page and the following screenshot:

By clicking on the link populated in the **View Original** column marked with a red outline, you have the option to review the original meeting recording. Only the original recording and last edited meeting recording are available for playback since Connect application will always have only these two versions.

Creating an offline recording

Now that you are familiar with reviewing a recording and editing it in order to eliminate parts when there were no actions in a meeting, we will show you how to create an offline recording. This feature is very useful in a case where you would like to review a recording without Internet access. In order to use this functionality, you must have Adobe Connect add-in installed in order to create an offline recording. To create an offline recording click on the **Make Offline** link in the desired recording row, as shown in the following screenshot:

When you create an offline recording for the first time, the **Offline Recording** dialog box will be displayed. If you don't want to see this message anymore, perform the following steps:

1. Click on the checkbox next to the label, **Don't show this message again**.

2. Click on the **Proceed with Offline Recording** button.

When you complete this action, you will be able to choose a download location for the selected recording. When you browse to the desired location, click on the **Save** button. By completing this action, you downloaded a chosen meeting recording and saved it to a selected location as a `.flv` file. Since you have downloaded this file for further review of the recording, you won't need Internet access or access to the Adobe Connect application. The only application needed to review the file is any available player that supports the FLV file format.

Summary

In this chapter we explained to you one of the essential Connect functionalities, meeting recordings. We guided you through the process of creation. During this chapter you have also passed different managing functionalities over the meeting recording and finally we taught you how to play back and edit recordings. So by now you should have a clear picture about built-in recording functionalities and how to use them. The next chapter will give you information on how you may use file share, web links, and poll pod inside a meeting room.

13
Sharing Files, Polls, and Web Links

After demonstrating recording functionalities in the previous chapter, once again we will visit the meeting room for additional guidelines. Just to remind you (in case you forgot), pods are visual component containers with defined functionalities. Starting from *Chapter 8, Using a Whiteboard Feature in the Meeting Room*, and continuing until *Chapter 10, Customizing Pod Display*, we described the share pod and its functionalities. In this chapter we will continue with the introduction of other pods. This chapter will focus on various functionalities of the file share pod, poll pod, and web links pod. At the end of this chapter you should have a sound knowledge on how to use the mentioned pods. This chapter will teach you how to use:

- File share pod
- Poll pod
- Web links pod

The file share pod

The first pod that we will introduce to you is the file share pod. The primary function of this pod is to share files among the meeting participants. The files can be uploaded to the file share pod, as well as downloaded from it. The important thing to mention in relation to a file share pod is that only hosts and presenters can upload files. In order to activate a file share pod, a user needs to follow the following steps:

1. Click on the **Pods** option in the meeting room main menu.
2. Then, click on the **Files** item in the meeting room's **Pods** menu.

After doing this, the user should be able to see the file share pod submenu.

This submenu contains two items that are available as options. By clicking on the **Add New File Share** menu item, a user can add an additional file share pod to an already running meeting in case there is a need for this. The upper-right corner of the next screenshot displays submenu content after the additional file share pod is added. After clicking on the **Files** menu item, you will activate the file share pod and it will appear in the meeting room, as shown in the following screenshot:

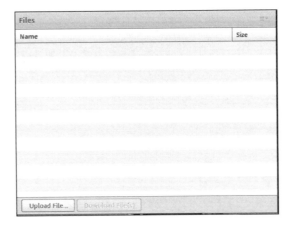

The file share pod consists of two columns: the first column is titled **Name** and it will display the name of the file; the second column is titled **Size**. The **Size** column shows the actual size of the shared file to a user. Just as with the functionality of the share pod, you can find the **Pod Options** button in the upper-right corner of the pod. When you click on this button, the **Pods** menu will appear and you will be able to choose among several options that are accessible. Now that we have gone through these basic functions of the file share pod, we will demonstrate to you how to upload, download, remove, and rename the chosen files.

Uploading a file

In order to upload a file located on your computer to the file share pod, a host or presenter will need to execute the following steps:

1. Click on the **Upload File...** button in the left-bottom part of the file share pod or click on the **Pod Options** button and select the **Upload File ...** menu option.

2. The **Select Document to Share** dialog box will be shown. This functionality was described in *Chapter 7, Sharing Presentations*.

3. Click on the **Browse My Computer...** button.

4. Navigate to the desired file that you would like to upload.

5. Click on the **Open** button.

6. By completing this, the file is uploaded and it should be visible inside the file share pod, as shown in the following screenshot:

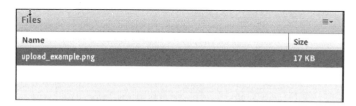

In addition to uploading a file from your computer as shown in the previous example, there are three additional options available in the the **Select Document to Share** dialog box. These options are: **Uploaded Files**, **Shared Content**, and **My Content**. You can read more details about the listed options in *Chapter 7, Sharing Presentations*. Meeting attendees with participant roles can add files inside the file share pod as well. In order to do this, they should have enhanced participant privileges assigned to this pod. A meeting host has the ability to grant them enhanced privileges.

Downloading a file

It is important to note that all meeting attendees have the right to download files from the file share pod without restrictions related to their meeting role. To download a file from the file share pod, a user should perform the following steps:

1. Select the chosen file inside file share pod. You can download several or all files using multiple selections (using the *Ctrl* or *Shift* keys).

2. Click on the **Download File(s)** button, which will be enabled when any file is uploaded. This button is located on the bottom-left part of the file share pod.

3. A new tab will be opened in your default browser, and you will need to locate the **Click to Download** link inside the newly opened page. Depending on the computer user settings, the browser tab may appear behind the meeting room. Then the user needs to look for it on its computer.

4. When you click on this link, you will see the dialog box the shown in the following screenshot:

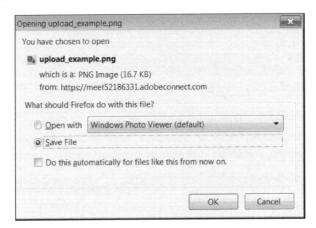

5. After you click on the **OK** button and select the radio button next to the **Save File** option, you will download the file to your default location on your computer.

In addition to downloading a single file, Adobe Connect supports downloading multiple files that are shared inside the file share pod. In the case where a user wants to download all of the shared files, the user can also click on the **Pod Options** button and select the **Download All** option from the pod options menu.

Removing a file

To remove a chosen file from the file share pod, users with adequate privileges will need to follow these steps:

1. Select the chosen file inside the file share pod.

2. Select the **Remove Selected** menu option from the pod option menu.

3. A confirmation dialog box will be displayed.

4. Click on the **Remove File(s)** button.

When you complete these steps, the selected file is successfully removed from the file share pod and it should be removed from the file list.

Renaming a file

This function changes the name of a selected file inside the file share pod, while it doesn't rename a file on your filesystem or in the Content library, in cases where that file was used for a previous upload. To change a filename inside the pod, you will need to perform the following steps:

1. Select the desired file inside the file share pod.

2. Click on the **Rename Selected** menu option from the pod option menu. The **Edit File Name** dialog will be shown.

3. Enter a new name for the selected file in the text field and click on the **OK** button.

4. With this example we finished the review of the file share pod all together with its functionalities, and now we can continue to the poll pod functionalities.

The poll pod

Another built-in pod type in the Connect application is the poll pod. The poll pod is very useful for hosts and presenters when they want to gather feedback from meeting attendees. The hosts and presenters have the ability to create different kind of polls (for example, multiple questions or multiple answers polls) and to review given results. The poll pod is initially visible in a meeting room when the **Discussion** layout or some other custom-made layout is used. In cases where you need to enable a poll pod (in addition to previously described ways you can access it) you should follow these steps:

1. Click on the **Pods** option in a meeting room main menu.

2. Click on the **Poll** item in a meeting room's **Pods** menu.

3. Click on the **Poll** submenu option.

    The following screenshot illustrates these steps:

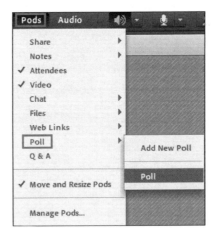

You can see that the option **Add New Poll** is present in the **Poll** submenu. This suggests that you can have as many polls inside a meeting room as you need. Once you click on the **Poll** submenu option, the poll pod will be added to a currently running meeting room. The poll pod should look like this:

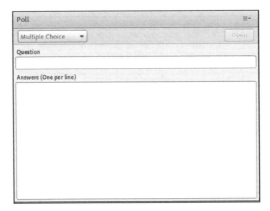

Our main point of interest for further feature explanation of this pod will be the drop-down menu, which gives a user the option to choose poll type as well as the **Pod Options** button. After you click on the **Pod Options** button, a pop-up menu will appear and you will find different functionalities associated with a poll. We will explain and guide you through these functionalities by going through a couple of examples.

Creating a poll

Before we create a poll, it is necessary to explain the differences among the three basic poll types. If a user creates a multiple questions poll, attendees can vote only for one of the offered options. The second case is where user creates multiple answers poll. Here, attendees can vote for multiple options that are offered. The third and the
final poll type is the short answer poll. In this poll attendees will need to provide a short answer to a presented question. Only presenters and hosts have the ability to create polls. In order to create a poll, users with adequate privileges should follow these steps:

1. In the drop-down menu in the upper-left part of the pod, choose the poll type you would like to create. The poll types that are offered are **Multiple Choice**, **Multiple Answers**, and **Short Answer**.

2. In the **Question** text field you will need to enter a question (for example, `What is your favorite color?`).

3. In cases where you didn't select the **Short Answer** poll type, you will need to enter answers in the text area. Answers should be entered one answer per single line (for example: add `red`, `green`, and `blue`). You can copy/paste your questions and answers from any notepad.

4. Now, the **Open** button should be enabled and you can click on it.

5. By completing this, you have opened your new poll for meeting attendees voting.

After a poll is created it can be closed after any period of time. When a poll is closed any additional changes to the votes will not be applied to a poll result. In order to close the poll for further votes, you will need to click on the **Close** button.

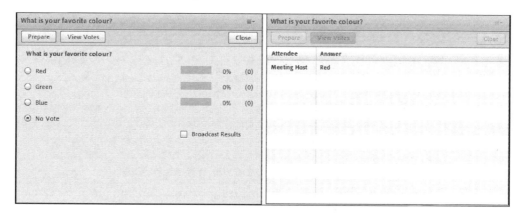

Showing voting results

In order to vote any meeting, attendees can click on their preferred option and changes in the poll will be applied immediately, as well as it will also be shown in the real time to hosts and presenters. In order to change how results are displayed, you can follow these steps:

1. Click on the **Pod Options** button in the upper-right corner.

2. Select the **Result Format** menu option.

3. Choose among one of the three options offered: **Show as %**, **Show as Numbers**, and **Show Both**.

If you would like to show the overall vote results to all meeting attendees including participants, you can click on the checkbox **Broadcast Results**. In order to see how a particular meeting attendee voted, you should click on the **View Votes** button. In the first column titled **Attendee**, you will find the attendee name, and in second column titled **Answer**, you will find submitted poll options for that user.

Editing polls

Once a poll is opened, you can edit it by following these steps:

1. Click on the **Prepare** button in the upper-right corner.

2. Add necessary changes to the poll.

3. Now, click again on the **Open** button.

The Poll pod functionalities are now covered. Note that hitting the **Prepare** button will reset the results. Beware of this during your polling sessions!

The web links pod

In cases where there is a need to give access to a specific web page to all meeting attendees inside a meeting, you should use the web links pod. Only hosts and presenters can copy/paste a URL in the chat pod. With just one click participants can open the web page in their default browsers. Initially this pod is not present inside a meeting room and, in order to add it, a user should follow these steps that are similar to the previous two cases:

1. Click on the **Pods** option in the meeting room main menu.

2. Click on the **Web Links** item in the meeting room's **Pods** menu.

3. Click on the **Add New Web Links** submenu option.

The previous screenshot illustrates previously described steps. Once this is completed, a web links pod should be present in a meeting room and it will be available for further usage. The **Web links 2** pod looks like the following screenshot:

This pod contains only two buttons: the first one is the **Browse To** button in the lower-left part of the window and second one is the **Pod Options** button in the upper-right part of the window. The commonly used functionalities in this pod are **Add Link**, **Remove Link**, **Rename Link**, and **Browse To**. We will describe them individually:

Adding link

To add a link to a web links pod, a user should complete the following steps:

1. Click on the Add Link... menu option from the pod option menu. The **Add Link** dialog will be shown.

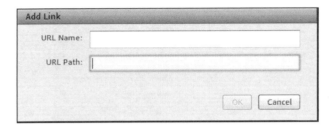

2. In the **URL Path** text field you will need to enter a URL address of the desired page (for example, www.google.com).

3. In the **URL Name** text field you will need to enter a name that best describes the entered web page (for example, Google).

4. Click on the **OK** button to add a link.

5. After you go through all of the mentioned steps, this link should be present inside the web links pod.

Displaying a web page

Once a web link is added to the web links pod to display the chosen page, the user should perform the following steps:

1. Select the link in the web links pod.

2. Once the link is selected, a URL address should be shown in the text field next to the **Browse To** button.

3. Click on the **Browse To** button.

4. This will automatically open your default browser and load your chosen page to all meeting attendees.

Renaming a link or changing a link's URL

In the case where a user realizes that there is a need to rename an already added link inside the web links pod, the user will need to complete the following steps to rename it:

1. Select a desired link that you would like to rename.

2. Choose the **Rename Selected Link...** item from the pod options menu.

3. This will open the **Modify Link** dialog, which looks exactly like the previously captured **Add Link**.

4. Here, a user can edit the link name or the URL address.

5. After clicking on the **OK** button, all changes will be saved permanently.

Removing a link

When user needs to remove an already added link from the web links pod, these steps need to be followed:

1. Select the chosen link.

2. Select the **Remove Selected** menu option from the pod options menu.

3. By doing this your link will be removed.

At this point we have gone through all of the functionalities of the web links pod, and we have completed describing functionalities associated with this pod.

Summary

In this chapter we explained frequently used functionalities such as file sharing, web links, and poll pods. You should be able to use these pods in everyday communication with confidence. In the next chapter you will learn how to manage text messages and questions using Chat, Notes, and Q&A pods.

14
Managing Text Messages and Questions

In this chapter we will continue introducing various meeting room pods to you. Throughout this chapter we will cover functionalities of the most common pods used in meeting conversations. This group consists of:

- Chat pod
- Notes pod
- Questions and answers pod (also named Q&A)

At the end of this chapter you should be completely confident about using the preceding pods.

Chat pod

We will start with chat pod functionality. If you used a default template when meeting was created, a chat pod will be initially available inside the meeting room and will be placed in the lower-right part of the meeting room. In case that you are using a custom-created template and if you are missing a chat pod, you will need to perform the following steps:

1. Click on the **Pods** menu in the meeting room main menu.
2. Click on the **Chat** item in the meeting room's **Pods** menu.
3. Click on one of the two offered options. You can click on **Chat** if you want to display a chat pod in the meeting room, or you can click on the **Add New Chat** menu item in order to add additional chat pod to a currently running meeting.

Regardless of how a chat pod is enabled, it will look exactly the same as the following screenshot:

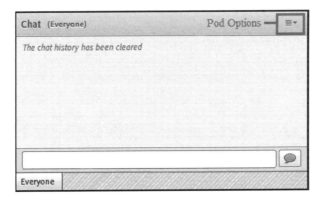

Chat pod is used for conversation between meeting attendees. By using chat pods, attendees can leave a message to a specific user, send a message to all attendees with particular roles such as presenters or hosts, and post public message to all meeting attendees. In order to create any of the three previously mentioned chat messages you should perform the following steps:

1. Select the **Start Chat With** option from the **Pod Options** menu.

2. In the submenu select a desired message recipient among the **Hosts**, **Presenters**, and **Attendees** options (for this example, we will select the **Hosts** option).

When you do so, a new tab will be added to the chat pod and will be highlighted, as shown in the following screenshot:

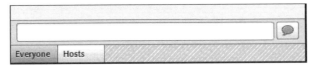

After you enter a message text in the text field, click on the **Send** button, or press the *Enter* key on your keyboard. The message will be sent and should be displayed inside the chat pod. In addition to this option you can also find options for text customization in the **Pod Options** menu. These options are as follows:

- **Text Size**: This option allows users to choose different font sizes for the chat pod text. Users can choose font size in the range from **8** to **72**.

- **My Chat Color**: This option provides users with an ability to change font color. The colors that are offered are **red**, **orange**, **green**, **brown**, **purple**, **pink**, **blue**, and **black**.

- **Show Timestamps**: This option is only available for a meeting host; by selecting this option a timestamp with the message time and date will be added to the chat pod and will be visible to all meeting attendees.

After sample customization changes are applied, the chat pod text area might look like the following screenshot:

Chat pod content is permanent, and it will stay in the chat pod regardless of how many times a meeting is closed or reopened until it is removed by a meeting host.

In order to remove chat content from the pod, perform the following steps:

1. From the **Pod Options** menu, select the **Clear Chat History** option.

2. You should be able to see a message in the chat pod – **The chat history has been cleared**.

In case when a host wants to save a chat history before removing content from the pod as described previously, the **Email Chat History** functionality should be utilized. This can be done by performing the following steps:

1. From the **Pod Options** menu select the **Email Chat History** option.

2. Once this is done, the host should be able to see a notification message in the upper-right part of the screen, as shown in the following screenshot:

By covering these options, we have covered all of the functionalities of the chat pod menu. In addition to these functionalities, you will find additional chat pod functionalities in the **Preferences** dialog box under the **Chat** section. You can access the **Preferences** dialog box by performing the following steps:

1. Click on the **Meeting** main menu option.

2. Click on the **Preferences** menu item.

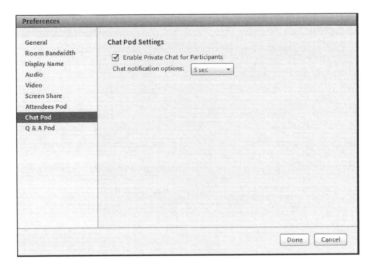

Here, users with a host role can find a checkbox to enable or disable private chat for participants and will find a drop-down menu to choose the time for chat notification messages. These messages are used when a user is in the screen share mode or if the meeting window is minimized and new messages arrive in the chat pod. In this case users will see a notification message similar to the message used in the **Email Chat History** functionality in the lower-right corner of the screen. By describing these items we covered all of the functionalities of a chat pod.

Notes pod

In a situation when there is a need to capture various meeting notes, to create particular meeting reminder, or to write an agenda to prepare for a meeting, hosts can rely on the notes pod. Hosts and presenters have read and write permissions over the notes pod while attendees only have read permissions by the default setting. Meeting hosts can create and display notes pod. To display or create one, they will need to perform the following steps:

1. Click on the **Pods** menu in the meeting room main menu.

2. Click on the **Notes** item in the meeting room's **Pods** menu.

3. Click on the **Notes** menu item or on the **Add New Note** menu item.

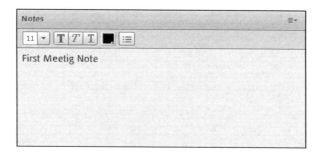

Hosts have the ability to add as many notes pods as they need. Notes pods can be resized and moved to any place inside a meeting room. To move the notes pod click on the title bar and drag the pod to your preferred position. In order to resize the pod, place your mouse pointer at any corner of the notes pod and drag it to resize it to a wanted size.

To add a note inside the notes pod simply click anywhere inside the text area and add text. The preceding screenshot shows the notes pod with a sample note entered. Once a note is added, it can be edited as well. To edit a note, perform the following steps:

1. Select the text inside the notes pod that you want to edit.

2. From the text toolbar, select the option to change the font color, size, or style.

3. Changes should be immediately applied to all meeting attendees.

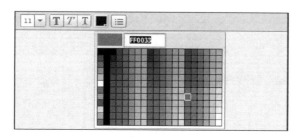

Hosts, presenters, and participants with additional administrative privileges for the notes pod will have the ability to edit already added notes. In case you have forgotten how to add enhanced privileges to a participant for any pod, you can review the steps, which are described in detail in *Chapter 6, Meeting Room Overview*. Once a note is added to the notes pod, it will remain there until the host deletes it. In the meantime, the host can switch between different pod layouts, but if the same pod is used, note that is added will be visible in the pod. Also, if the host decides to end and restart a meeting, same note will remain visible to meeting attendees.

In order to avoid this situation, hosts can use different notes pods for different layouts. If for some reason hosts would like to save notes before deleting them, the **Export Note** functionality should be used. This functionality is available under the **Pod Options** menu. Users can choose between two options for saving a specific note: **Email Note ...**, which will e-mail a note to an entered e-mail recipient or **Save as Rtf ...**, which will save the selected note in the `.rtf` format. `.rtf` files can easily be opened with Microsoft Word or any other word processor software.

Now that we are finished with options that enable users to download pod content, we will explain how to delete previously added notes pods. To complete this operation users should perform the following steps:

1. Click on **Pods** in the meeting room main menu.
2. Click on the **Manage Pods** menu option.
3. The **Manage Pods** dialog box will be displayed.
4. Select the desired notes pod you want to remove.
5. Click on the **Delete** button in the **Manage Pods** dialog box.
6. By executing this, you will permanently remove the desired notes pod.

After examining how you can delete and permanently remove the note pod from a meeting room, we have finished describing this pod and will continue by describing the questions and answers pod.

Q&A pod

This is the last pod, which we will cover in this chapter. The Q&A pod is very useful in situations where participants have the need to raise questions related to presented meeting content. In a case where a user doesn't want to interrupt presentation, it is useful to display the Q&A pod in a meeting room and to allow participants to ask questions by using this feature. Once when a presentation is completed, the presenter can review participants' questions in the Q&A pod and start to answer individual questions or all of them at once. Once when the presenter provides an answer for a question, both question and answer will be shown as a single group to all meeting attendees. In order to display Q&A pod inside a meeting you must have the host role and perform the following steps:

1. Click on the **Pods** menu in the meeting room main menu.

2. Click on the **Q&A** menu item.

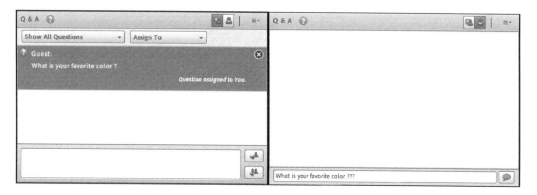

As you can see in the preceding screenshots, this pod has two views. Meeting attendees with the participant role will see this pod as shown in the screenshot on the right-hand side. As you can see, participants only have the ability to ask questions during a presentation. In order to ask a particular question, participants should enter text inside the text field and click on the **Send Question** button. The **Send Question** button is placed on the right-hand side of the text field. Questions can also be submitted inside the Q&A pod by pressing the *Enter* key on your keyboard. When submitted, the question will be added to the Q&A pod, and users with a host or presenter role will be able to review it. The Q&A pod appearance for hosts and presenters is shown in the left-hand screenshot from the preceding two screenshots. In addition to the capability to see questions from attendees, users with a host or presenter role can use additional options. One of the options available is to delegate the question to a specific meeting attendee. To do this, you will need to perform the following steps:

1. Click on the **Assign To** drop-down list.

2. Select the desired meeting attendee from the drop-down list.

3. You should be able to see the message **Question assigned to**, followed by the attendee name, as shown in the following screenshot:

An attendee who needs to provide an answer to the assigned question can choose between the following two options when responding:

- **Send Privately**: Use this option when you want to respond to a question only to the person who asked it. It is displayed as ⬚.

- **Send To All**: Use this option when you want to provide the answer to all of meeting attendees. It is displayed as ⬚.

Once the answer is provided, it will be assigned to the original question, as shown in the following screenshot:

Guest: What is your favorite color ?
Meeting Presenter(privately): My favorite color is RED

The preceding screenshot shows how the answer provided for a specific question will be displayed to a participant. The following screenshot shows how a private answer will be displayed to a presenter or host:

Inside the Q&A pod, users can find a drop-down list that is used to filter questions based on the following listed options:

- **Show All Questions**: By selecting this option, all questions will be displayed

- **Show Open Questions**: By selecting this option, only questions that are not answered will remain visible inside the pod

- **Show Answered Questions**: This option displays all the questions that are answered

- **Show My Questions**: This option displays all of the questions assigned to a specific user

These options are shown in the following screenshot:

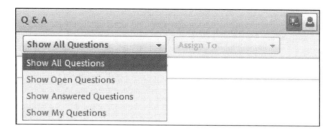

In addition to the already described features under the **Pod Options** menu, you can find common features that were previously described and some specific Q&A pod features. Specific Q&A features are **Remove All Questions** and **Export Q&A Log**. The first feature clears all of the questions from the Q&A pod and the second feature helps you download pod content as a .rtf file or e-mail pod content. The following options are available in the **Q&A** section of the **Preferences** dialog box:

- **Show Submitter Name With Answered Question**
- **Show Presenter Name With Answered Question**

You can overview how to access the **Preferences** dialog box from the *Chat pod* section. These options are enabled or disabled by clicking on the checkbox next to their name labels.

By going through these functionalities, we have covered most of the functionalities of the questions and answers pod.

Summary

In this chapter you have learned how to use three new pods. You learned how to use chat functionalities that the Connect meeting room provides you. Also, you have been introduced to taking notes during meetings using notes pod. We have covered most of the functionalities that a Q&A pod provides you. Now you are familiarized with asking and answering questions during a meeting without interrupting the meeting workflow. The next chapter will teach you how to create meetings that contain audio conference details and how to use video pod.

15
Using Audio and Video

Adobe Connect supports several solutions for adding audio and video to meetings. Throughout this chapter you will be learning how to start audio and video conferences within meeting rooms. We will show you how to make and use Universal Voice audio providers and how to use integrated audio adapters without Universal Voice. You will also learn how to connect to video telephony streams and how to share webcam video.

In this chapter we will go through the following audio and video conferencing features:

- Using audio conferencing
- Creating and using an audio profile
- Starting an audio conference
- Managing audio within meetings
- Adjusting audio quality
- Using video pods

In this chapter we will focus on using integrated adapters. In order to go through the steps in this chapter, it is necessary to have contracted audio services with one of the audio conferencing providers that integrate with Connect (MeetingOne, InterCall, Arkadin, and PGi). You will also need to have audio conferencing credentials.

Using audio conferencing

In the meeting room, audio is broadcasted by using **voice over Internet protocol (VoIP)** and the microphones of attendee' computer systems. There are two options for integrating audio in the meeting – you can use Universal Voice audio providers or integrated audio adapters without Universal Voice.

Using integrated adapters

Integrated adapters, which are Adobe Connect extensions written in Java, provide communication between Adobe Connect and specific audio conferencing providers. Integrated adapters have advanced call capabilities, allowing hosts and presenters to control the audio conference from a meeting. Adobe provides several integrated telephony adaptors for hosted installations. For example, MeetingOne, PGi, and InterCall are integrated telephony adapters. Integrated adapters in licensed installations can also be configured for Universal Voice.

Hosts have several options for dialing out to include participants in an audio conference call. You can dial out to a registered participant by using the telephone number stored in his/her profile or by entering a new telephone number. To include an unregistered participant in the audio conference call only, you can enter a new name and add his/her number to dial.

Creating and using an audio profile

An audio profile is a collection of audio conference settings that map to an audio provider. You can use audio profiles whenever you use an audio provider with a Connect meeting. Audio providers are companies that offer audio conferencing services that work with the Adobe Connect application.

All audio profiles include the audio provider and a profile name. The remaining information includes numbers and access codes that hosts provide for meetings. Then, the information requested depends on the provider. For integrated providers, the requested information comes from their configuration code.

In order to create a new audio provider, click on the **My Profile** link in the upper-right corner of the Adobe Connect web application and then click on the **My Audio Profiles** tab. You will be presented with the list of available audio profiles that were created by you. When you click on the **New Profile** button, the audio profile creation page will open, as shown in the following screenshot:

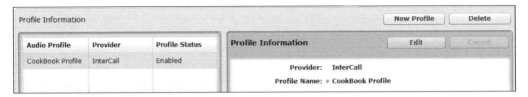

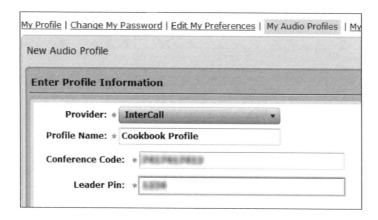

Meeting hosts, limited administrators, and administrators can create audio profiles.

Select an audio provider and name the profile. The following two fields are present for every audio provider:

- **Provider**: This drop-down list has audio providers configured for Universal Voice by an account administrator or host. Selecting a provider binds the audio profile to the information configured for the provider.

- **Profile Name**: This will contain a unique name that represents something meaningful to you, such as the purpose of the audio profile.

The remaining information depends on integrated audio adapter type. For example, for the InterCall adapter you will need to enter information in the **Conference Code** and **Leader Pin** fields. Fill in the remaining information and click on the **Save** button. Saving the profile automatically enables it for future use.

Editing or deleting an audio profile

You can change a profile name, and enable or disable an existing audio profile. You cannot change the audio provider and you can specify a provider only when you create a profile.

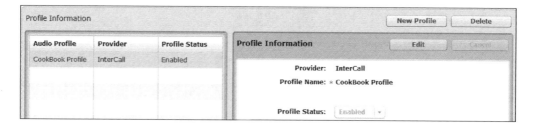

In order to change a profile, select a profile and click on the **Edit** button. Change the profile name or status and click on the **Save** button. In order to delete an audio profile, select it and click on the **Delete** button.

Associating an audio profile with a meeting

The next step is to associate the created audio profile with your meeting. In order to complete this action, select the **Include this audio conference with this meeting** option on the meeting creation page in the **Audio Conference Settings** section, and from the drop-down menu select the previously created profile (see the following screenshot).

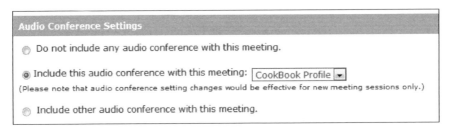

Please note that if you would like to change the audio profile associated with the meeting you must restart a meeting in order to apply new conferencing settings.

After you have associated an audio profile with the meeting, you can start an audio conference that integrates with Adobe Connect.

Starting an audio conference

In this section we will learn how to enable audio in the meeting. Also you will see what the basic steps to start an audio conference are.

Starting meeting audio

By default, the audio option for the meeting is disabled. In order to enable audio for the meeting you must perform the following steps:

1. From the **Audio** menu, choose one of the following options:

   ° **Microphone Rights for Participants**: This option appears if there is no audio profile attached to a meeting. Choose this option in order to enable an audio conference that uses VoIP.

- ○ **Start Meeting Audio**: This option appears if an audio profile is attached to a meeting.

2. You must also specify how you would like for attendees to join the meeting's audio conference. You can specify one or more options. The availability of the options depend on the meeting's audio and system configuration (please see the following screenshot).

The following are the available options:

- ○ **Using Computers**: Select this option if you would like for attendees to join the audio conference by using their computer speakers and microphones (VoIP). All users can hear meeting audio using the computer's speakers. To enable participants to speak, check the **Enable microphone rights for participants** checkbox.

- ○ **Using Phone**: Select this option if you would like for attendees to join the audio conference over the telephone. Users can dial in to the audio conference or receive a call from a meeting. Check the **Start broadcasting telephony audio** checkbox in order to enable attendees using computers to interact with attendees on phones.

3. After selecting one of the preceding options click on the **Start** button. Once the meeting audio has been started, attendees will need to join the audio conference.

Joining an audio conference

After a host starts an audio conference, a notification window appears in front of all attendees. Afterwards, they can broadcast their voices via their telephones or computer microphones.

In order to connect to conference audio, click on the **Telephone** button, which is displayed as 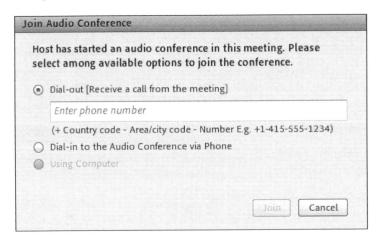 in the main menu bar. You will be presented with the **Join Audio Conference** dialog box. This box also appears when people log in to the conference once **Start Meeting Audio** is activated. (please see the following screenshot).

In this dialog box, select the **Dial-out [Receive a call from the meeting]** option in order to receive a call from the meeting on the telephone number you entered, or select the **Dial-in to the Audio Conference via Phone** option in order to place a call via telephone by using the number and instructions provided in the textbox.

If a dial-in token is provided, hosts can mute chosen attendees. Without a dial-in token, hosts must merge attendees with the related phone number in the attendees pod.

Managing audio within meetings

By default, in the meeting room, only hosts and presenters can broadcast audio by using their microphones. However, hosts can enable participants to broadcast audio by checking the **Enable microphone rights for participants** checkbox in the **Audio** menu. Hosts can also enable audio for specific participants by selecting one or more of the participants in the attendees pod and choose any of the options from the pop-up menu such as **Enable Audio**, **Make Host**, or **Make Presenter**, as shown in the following screenshots:

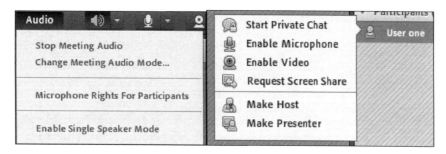

After selecting one of these options, a microphone icon will appear next to the attendee name, as shown in the following screenshot:

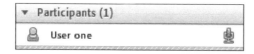

By using the same pop-up menu, hosts can later disable audio for selected attendees.

A Connect meeting room also provides you with an option to avoid overlapping conversations by selecting the **Enable Single Speaker Mode** option from the **Audio** menu.

When you select this option, an asterisk will appear next to the microphone button in the main menu bar. When one speaker clicks on the button, it is disabled for other users until the current speaker clicks on the button again.

Each attendee can manage their microphones and speakers. In addition to the microphone and speaker icons in the meeting room main menu, you will find a drop-down menu icon with additional options.

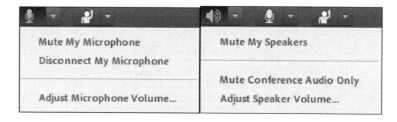

There are options to mute your speakers and microphones. You can also adjust your microphone and speaker volume by selecting the **Adjust Microsoft Volume...** and **Adjust Speaker Volume...** options, respectively. When you select this option, a volume slider will appear. Attendees can drag a slider to customize the volume, as shown in the following screenshots:

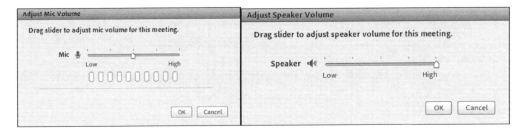

During longer meeting breaks, hosts may want to stop broadcasting audio. In order to do this, select **Stop Audio Broadcast** from the **Audio** menu. To resume audio broadcast you will need to select **Start Audio Broadcast** from the **Audio** menu. Please note that hosts can stop a broadcast for all attendees, but not for a specific participant. To stop an audio conference, click on **Stop Meeting Audio** from the **Audio** menu.

Adjusting audio quality

The Adobe Connect meeting room allows you to quickly optimize settings by using **Audio Setup Wizard**. To complete quick optimization, click on the **Audio Setup Wizard** option in the meeting menu. You will be presented with the **Audio Setup Wizard** dialog box, as shown in the following screenshot:

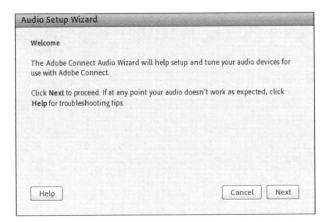

Follow the onscreen instructions to optimize the audio quality. If a dialog box appears requesting access to your camera and microphone, click on the **Allow** button.

To set advanced audio options from the meeting menu, select the **Preferences** option. In the displayed **Preferences** dialog box, click on the **Audio** tab in the left pane.

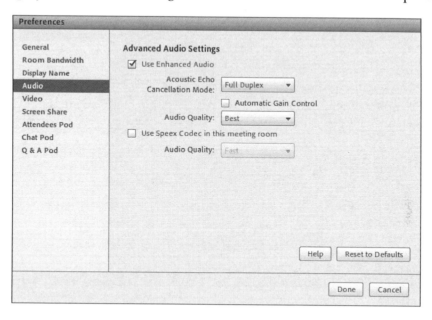

Check the **Use Enhanced Audio** checkbox to automatically cancel echoes, control microphone volume, and suppress noise. Uncheck this checkbox if you have problems with the audio quality.

For **Acoustic Echo Cancellation Mode**, three different options are offered, as follows:

- **Full Duplex**: This enables multiple users to speak at once. If echo feedback is created, select another option (this option is preferred for most systems).

- **Half Duplex**: This enables only one user to speak at a time. Use this option if microphones on your system are unusually sensitive (transmitting unwanted background sound) or if you have poor echo cancellation.

- **Headphones**: This optimizes audio settings for use with headphones. This option uses the **Full Duplex** mode, in which multiple users can speak at once.

In order to enable your microphone volume to adjust automatically in response to changes in the voice level, check the **Automatic Gain Control** checkbox. You can also set the audio quality by selecting one of the options available in the **Audio Quality** combo box. Those options are as follows:

- **Fast**: This provides the fastest performance but the lowest audio quality (use this option for systems with slower CPUs).

- **Best**: This provides the slowest performance but the best audio quality (use this option for systems with fast CPUs).

- **Custom**: This enables you to select options for audio quality settings. Use this option if the standard settings do not provide adequate results. Selecting this option displays some additional settings, as shown in the following screenshot:

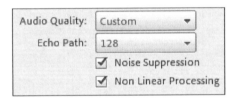

For **Echo Path**, select **128** (default setting) or **256**. The higher setting provides greater level of suppression for audio feedback. This setting uses more CPU resources and it is recommended for systems that don't use headphones.

Check **Noise Suppression** to reduce the amount of noise that your microphone can pick up. Uncheck this checkbox to make your microphone more sensitive.

Check the **Non Linear Processing** checkbox (selected by default) to use nonlinear processing for audio data. Uncheck this checkbox to use standard processing (and fewer CPU resources).

Select **Use Speex Codec** to take advantage of this VoIP-optimized technology (this option requires attendees to install the Adobe Connect add-in). Options range from **Fast** for fastest performance and poorest quality to **Best** for slowest performance and best quality.

Using video pods

By default, in the meeting room only hosts and presenters can broadcast video. However, hosts can enable broadcasting by participants to broadcast by selecting the **Enable Webcam For Participants** option in the drop-down menu next to the camera icon, which is displayed as 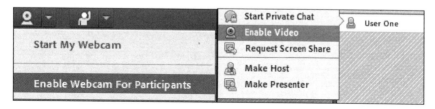. Hosts can also enable audio for specific participants by selecting one or more participants in the attendees pod and choosing any of the options such as **Enable Video**, **Make Host**, or **Make Presenter** from the pop-up menu, as shown in the following screenshots:

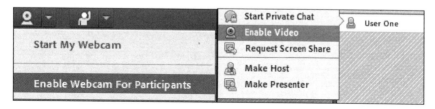

Hosts, presenters, and participants with enhanced user privileges can simultaneously share video from webcams connected to their computers.

If you are a host, presenter, or participant with video rights, you can adjust the quality of your webcam video.

To perform this, click on the menu icon in the upper-right corner of the video pod, and choose the **Preferences** option from the context menu of the video pod. You will be presented with the **Preferences** dialog box and the **Video** tab will be selected automatically, as shown in the following screenshot:

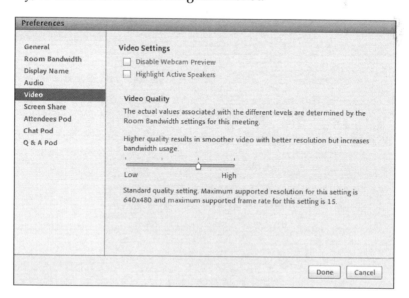

You can adjust the **Video Quality** setting to optimize the trade-off between image quality and bandwidth usage. For example, if shared screens update slowly, choose a lower **Video Quality** setting.

Sharing a video

In order to start sharing your webcam, click on the **Start My Webcam** button in the main menu bar of the **Video** pod.

In the **Video** pod, a preview image appears, so you can adjust your camera position. If you want to use a different camera that is connected, you can select it from the **Video** pod menu.

If you want to cancel video sharing, click outside the preview image in the **Video** pod. After clicking on the **Start Sharing** button your video will start to broadcast to all of the participants.

To pause or stop a video, hover the mouse over the **Video** pod, and click on the **Pause** or **Stop** icon.

When video is paused, the last image broadcasted from your camera remains static in the **Video** pod until you click on the **Play** button. When video is stopped, the broadcast image disappears entirely. Hosts can pause or stop a video from any attendee.

Summary

During this chapter we have covered most of the functionalities for audio and video conferencing options that an Adobe Connect meeting room provides. You have learned how to create audio providers and how to use integrated audio adapters. We have gone through the process of creating audio profiles and associating them with the Adobe Connect meeting. During this chapter we have familiarized you with starting audio conferences and managing audio and video during meetings.

16
Using Breakout Rooms

In this chapter we will go through the process of creating and using breakout rooms inside meeting. Breakout rooms can be defined as sub-rooms that users can create within a meeting room session. Creating breakout rooms allows you to easily split a large group of attendees into smaller groups. Breakout rooms can be used in meeting sessions that have 200 or more attendees. For a single meeting session you can create a maximum of 20 breakout rooms.

For a meeting session that has audio conference running, a host can create a certain number of breakout rooms depending on the number supported by the audio provider. Also if the number of users in breakout room exceeds the maximum supported number, breakout rooms can't be started.

Hosts can also end breakout sessions and return all attendees back to the main room. Also, a host is allowed to share breakout room activity with all attendees. You can also use the same breakout rooms with previously defined layouts and contents. Information about attendees' assignments to a room won't be preserved, so you will need to assign them all over again.

This chapter will introduce breakout rooms and their features to the user. It will cover the following topics:

- Defining breakout rooms and assigning members
- Beginning a breakout session
- Communication in breakout rooms

Defining breakout rooms and assigning members

Information about breakout rooms is placed within attendees pod of meeting. In the attendees pod you will find three tabs for attendees pod view. See the following screenshot:

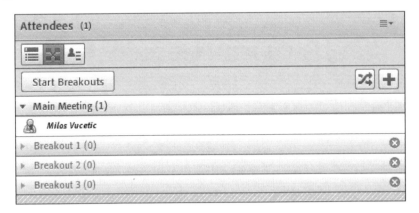

To define breakout rooms and assign members to them, perform the following steps:

1. Click on the **Breakout Room View** button, which is displayed as ![icon]. The attendees pod view will change and you will be presented with the information on available breakout rooms. Please note that only attendees with host rights can view this option in the attendees pod.

2. By default three breakout rooms are available in the breakout view. You can easily create breakout rooms by clicking on the **Create a New Breakout** button, which is displayed as ![icon].

3. When you have reached the number of breakout rooms that fits your needs, you can now begin assigning attendees to selected breakout rooms. There are two ways to do this.

   ○ You can select an attendee name from the list of attendees and drag it to the desired breakout room using your mouse or select the breakout room from the pop-up menu. You can also select several attendees from the list by using *Ctrl* + click or *Shift* + click to select multiple attendees. See the following screenshot:

- ° You can also assign attendees to breakout rooms by clicking on **Evenly Distribute from Main**, which is displayed as ⬚. This option will simply assign all attendees to breakout rooms adding them user by user to different breakout rooms. Please note that already assigned users will stay in the same rooms.

4. Hosts can remove breakout rooms by clicking on the **X** button in the upper-right corner of the breakout room in the attendees pod. Please note that the number of breakout rooms will change in order to ensure continuity. There is also an option to remove all breakout rooms by clicking on **Remove All Rooms...** from the **Attendees Pod** menu. See the following screenshot:

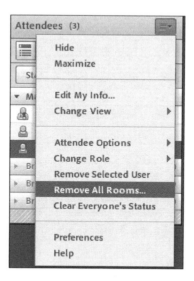

5. After you have finished with the creation of breakout rooms and attendees' assignments to rooms, you can start your breakout session.

Beginning a breakout session

In order to start the breakout room session you will need to click on the **Start Breakouts** button. By clicking on this button, a notification message will appear, signalizing that you have started the breakout session.

Attendees are placed in the breakout rooms according to assignments done by the host. By default all attendees have presenter rights so they can share their voice, share content in the share pod, modify whiteboards, and add text to the notes pod. All attendees in the breakout rooms can download shared content – even the users who entered the meeting as guests. When the host returns users to the main meeting room, attendees' roles will be reverted to default ones.

The host can visit each of the active breakout rooms by simply dragging his name from the attendee list pod to a desired breakout room. It is very important to not display the participants pod in the presenters only area before starting the breakout rooms since this area will be hidden in the sub-rooms.

Communication within breakout session

Users can chat within their breakout room using a chat pod. Communication between attendees from different breakout rooms is not possible. For hosts there is an option to broadcast message to all attendees placed in the different breakout rooms. To do this click on the **Broadcast Message...** option from the **Attendees Pod** menu. You will be presented with the input field where you can type your message, as shown in the following screenshots:

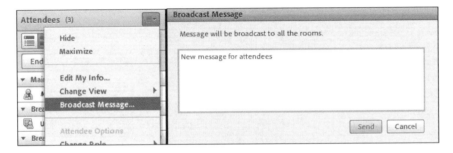

After you click on the **Send** button, attendees in all rooms receive a message, which gets displayed at the center of their screens. This can be useful if you have noticed a similar question in several breakout rooms. In order to avoid breaking current user activities such as chat, file loading, and other user activities within the breakout rooms, a few minutes before ending breakout sessions you can send a warning message to attendees in breakout rooms. It is also a good practice to return users to the main room.

Breakout rooms also provide you with an option to post different polls to different rooms. To do this just go to the desired room and open a poll pod from the **Pods** menu.

Attendees in breakout rooms can ask the host whether the host is in their breakout room or not at any time. In the **Chat Pod** menu select the **Send a message to host** option. The host can respond in the chat pod to an attendee alone or can answer to everyone.

An attendee can also broadcast a question to all hosts in the meeting by entering the message in the **Send a message to host** text field. After clicking on the **Send** button, all hosts will be presented with the message displayed in the box along with the attendee name in it. See the following screenshots:

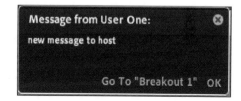

Ending a breakout session

Only users with host rights can end a breakout session. Closing breakout rooms will return all attendees to the main meeting room. In order to end the breakout session click on the **End Breakouts** button in the breakout view of attendees pod.

Sharing breakout room content in the main room

Hosts are also provided with the ability to share the contents of a specific breakout room with everyone in the main room even after the breakout session is ended. To do this go to the **Breakout Pods** submenu of the **Pods** menu, as shown in the following screenshot:

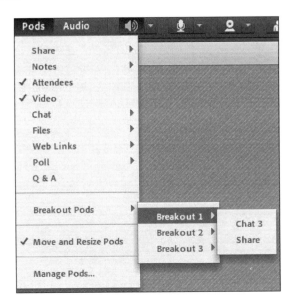

Select a breakout room name from which you want to share content. You can now select the pod of your choice in order to show it to all attendees. The new pod will open with selected content inside it. The contents cannot be changed or edited.

Reopening breakout rooms

In the attendees pod, click on the **Breakout Room View** button. You can again add rooms or change attendees' assignments before you start the breakout session again. Now click on the **Start Breakouts** button in order to start the breakout session again. Please note that all rooms' configurations as well as the list of assigned users will remain the same.

Summary

In this chapter you have learned how to use the breakout rooms feature of a meeting. You can now mange users within different breakout rooms. The next chapter will teach you how to use external applications closely tied to Adobe Connect such as Adobe Connect Outlook Add-in and Adobe Connect Add-in for Microsoft Lync.

Index

About Packt Publishing

Packt, pronounced 'packed', published its first book "*Mastering phpMyAdmin for Effective MySQL Management*" in April 2004 and subsequently continued to specialize in publishing highly focused books on specific technologies and solutions.

Our books and publications share the experiences of your fellow IT professionals in adapting and customizing today's systems, applications, and frameworks. Our solution based books give you the knowledge and power to customize the software and technologies you're using to get the job done. Packt books are more specific and less general than the IT books you have seen in the past. Our unique business model allows us to bring you more focused information, giving you more of what you need to know, and less of what you don't.

Packt is a modern, yet unique publishing company, which focuses on producing quality, cutting-edge books for communities of developers, administrators, and newbies alike. For more information, please visit our website: www.packtpub.com.

Writing for Packt

We welcome all inquiries from people who are interested in authoring. Book proposals should be sent to author@packtpub.com. If your book idea is still at an early stage and you would like to discuss it first before writing a formal book proposal, contact us; one of our commissioning editors will get in touch with you.

We're not just looking for published authors; if you have strong technical skills but no writing experience, our experienced editors can help you develop a writing career, or simply get some additional reward for your expertise.

Adobe Flash 11 Stage3D
(Molehill) Game Programming

A step-by-step guide for creating stunning 3D games in
Flash 11 Stage3D (Molehill) using AS3 and AGAL

Beginner's Guide

Christer Kaitila

Adobe Flash 11 Stage3D (Molehill) Game Programming Beginner's Guide

ISBN: 978-1-849691-68-0   Paperback: 412 pages

A step-by-step guide for creating stunning 3D games
in Flash 11 Stage3D (Molehill) using AS3 and AGAL

1. The first book on Adobe's Flash 11 Stage3D,
   previously codenamed Molehill

2. Build hardware-accelerated 3D games with a
   blazingly fast frame rate.

3. Full of screenshots and ActionScript 3 source
   code, each chapter builds upon a real-world
   example game project step-by-step.

Adobe Edge
Quickstart Guide

Quickly produce engaging motion and rich interactivity
with Adobe Edge Preview 4 and above

Joseph Labrecque   PACKT

Adobe Edge Quickstart Guide

ISBN: 978-1-849693-30-1   Paperback: 136 pages

Quickly produce engaging motion and rich
interactivity with Adobe Edge Preview 4 and above

1. Learn to use Adobe's newest application to
   create engaging motion and rich interactivity

2. Familiarize yourself with the Edge interface
   and unleash your creativity through standard
   HTML, CSS, and JavaScript

3. Add motion and interactivity to your websites
   using Web standards

4. A quickstart guide for creating engaging
   content with Adobe Edge

Please check **www.PacktPub.com** for information on our titles

Made in the USA
San Bernardino, CA
15 January 2016